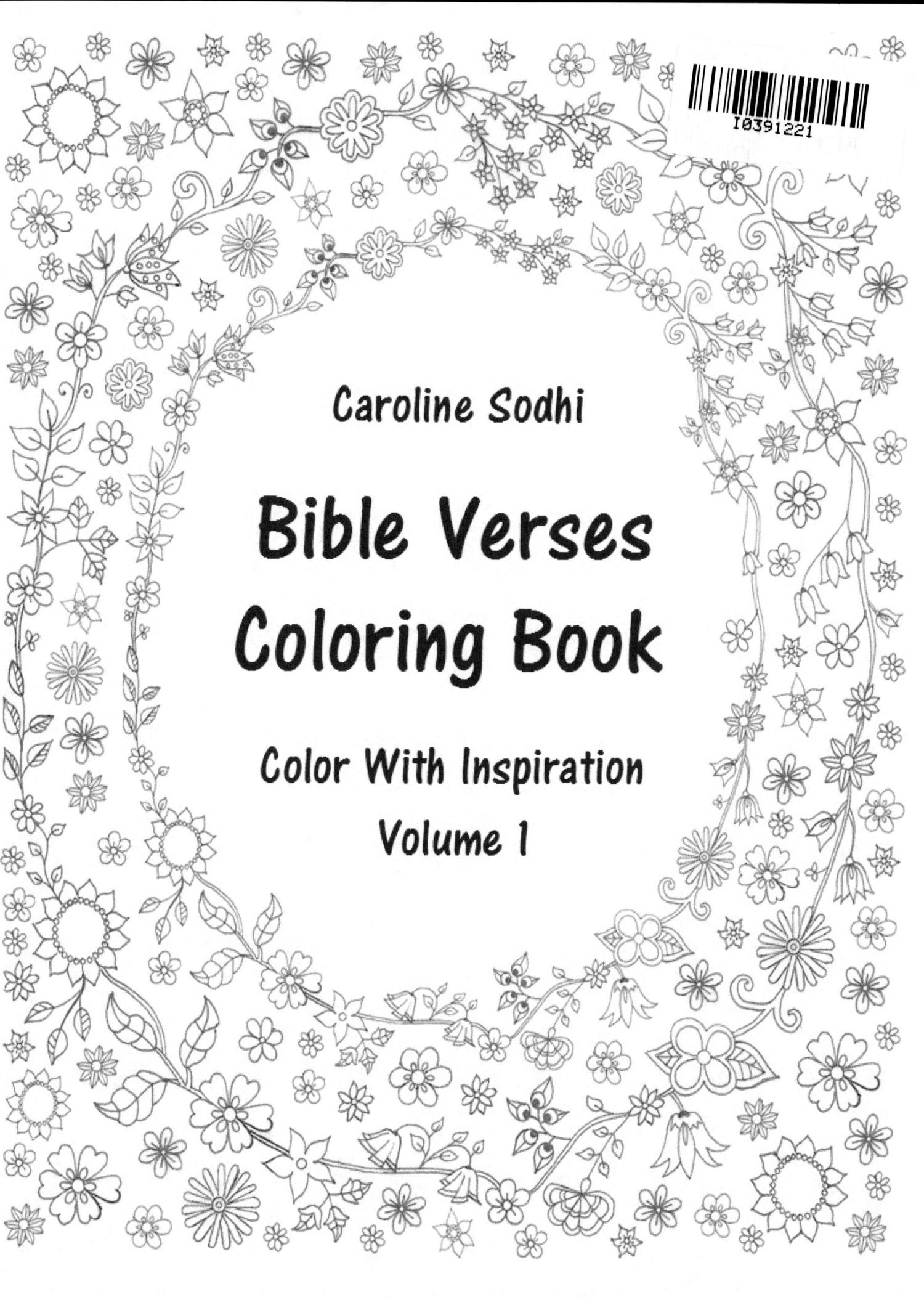

Caroline Sodhi

Bible Verses Coloring Book

Color With Inspiration

Volume 1

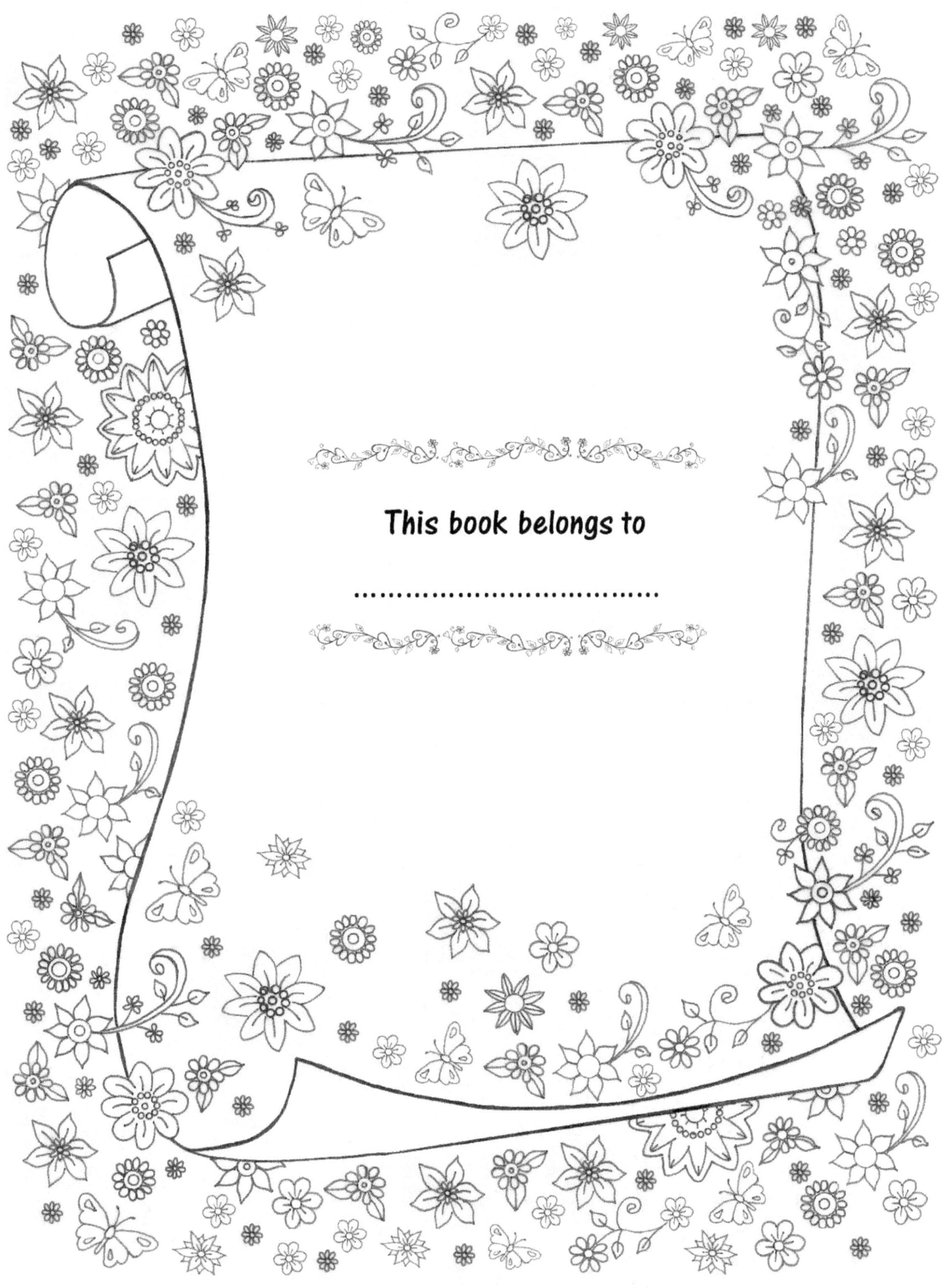

This book belongs to

....

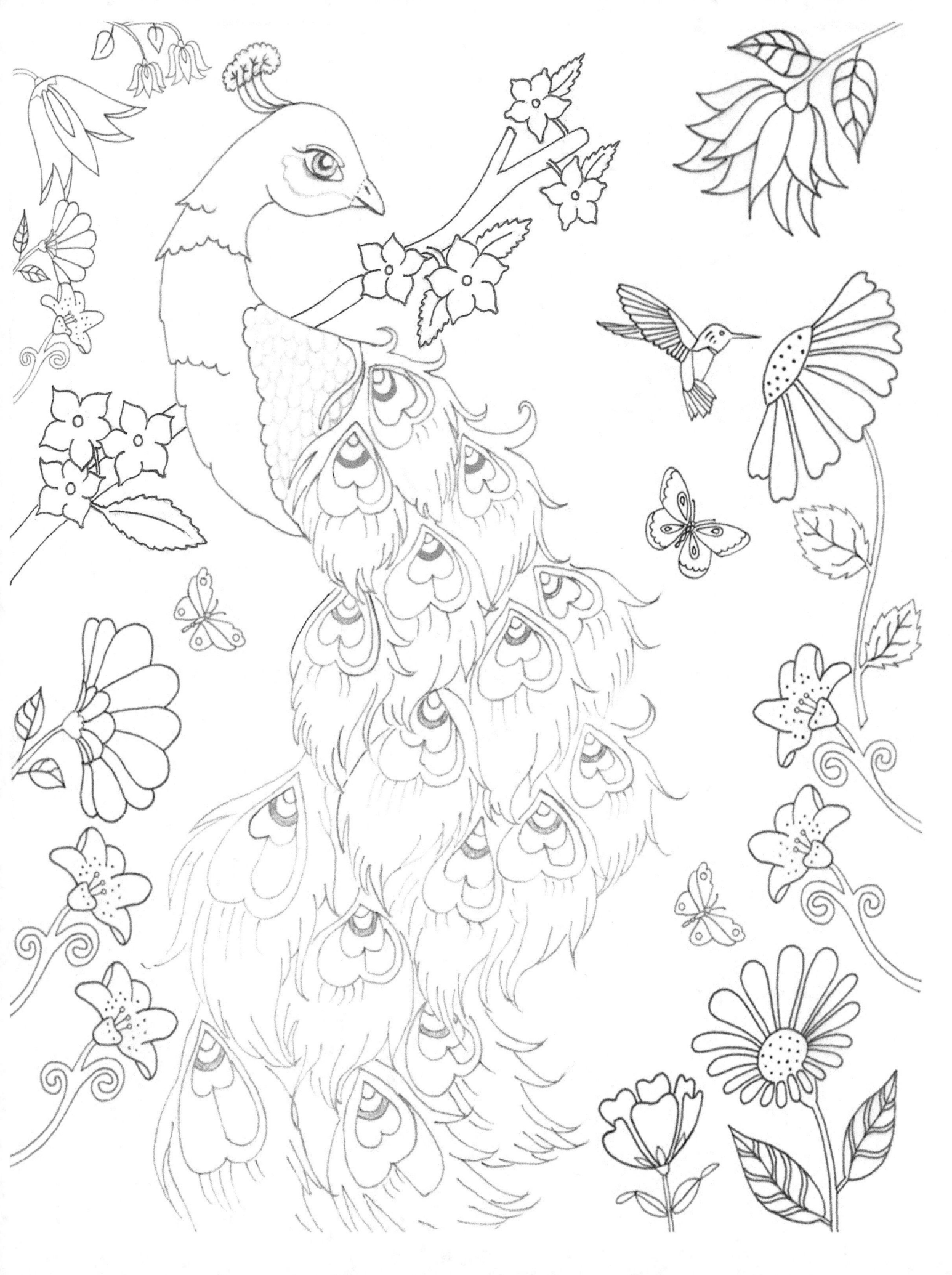

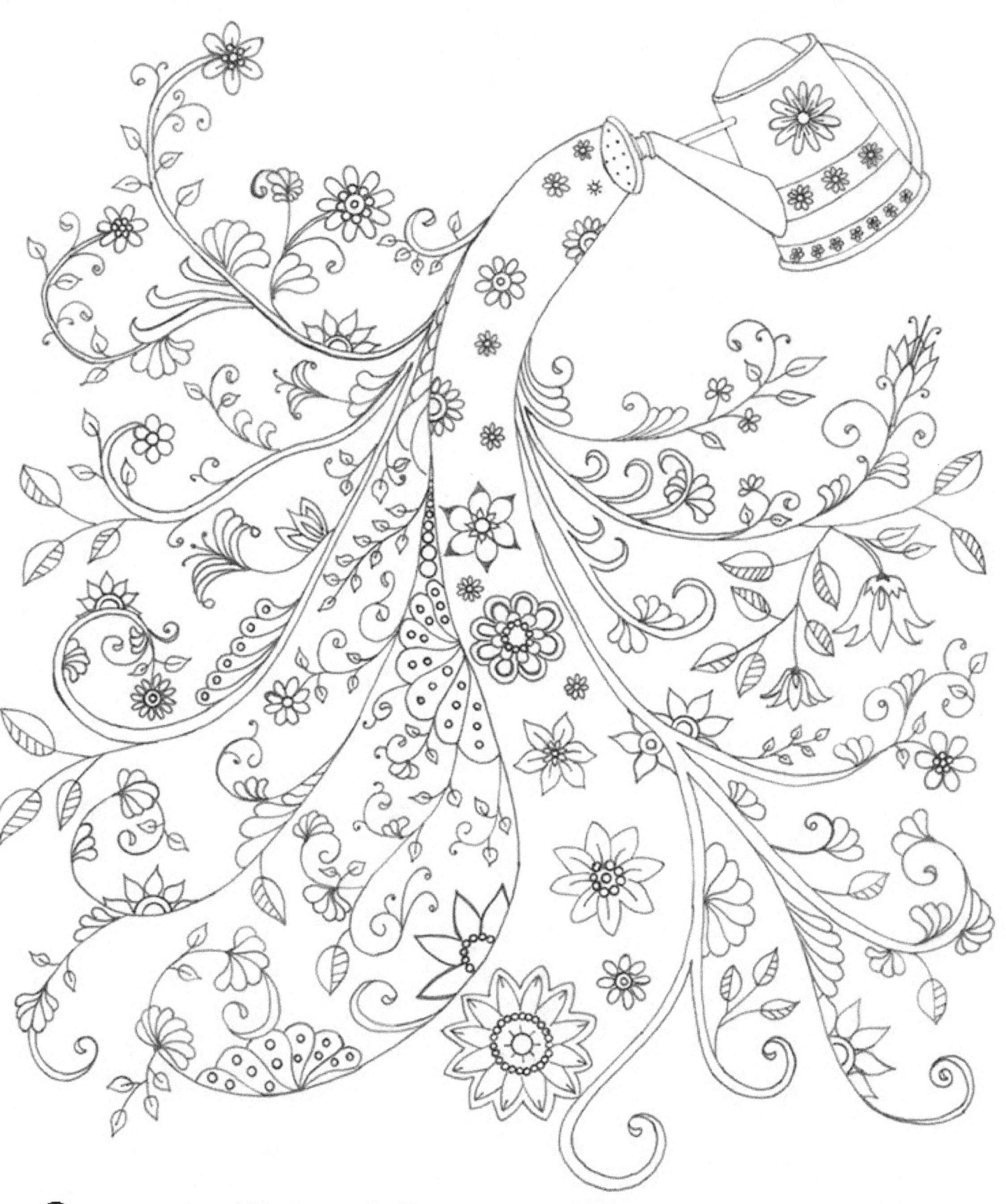

You will be like a well-watered garden,
like a spring whose waters never fail.

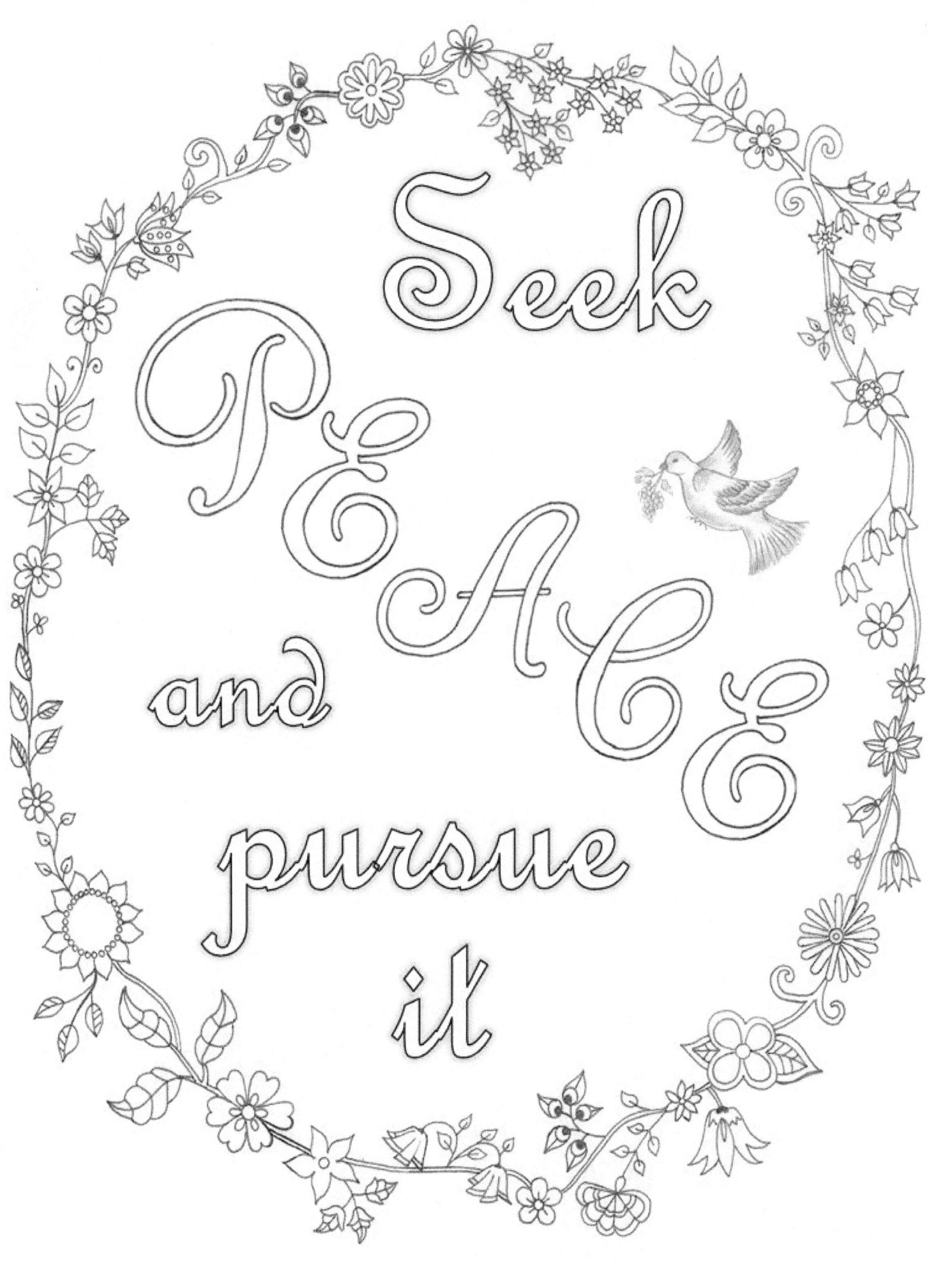

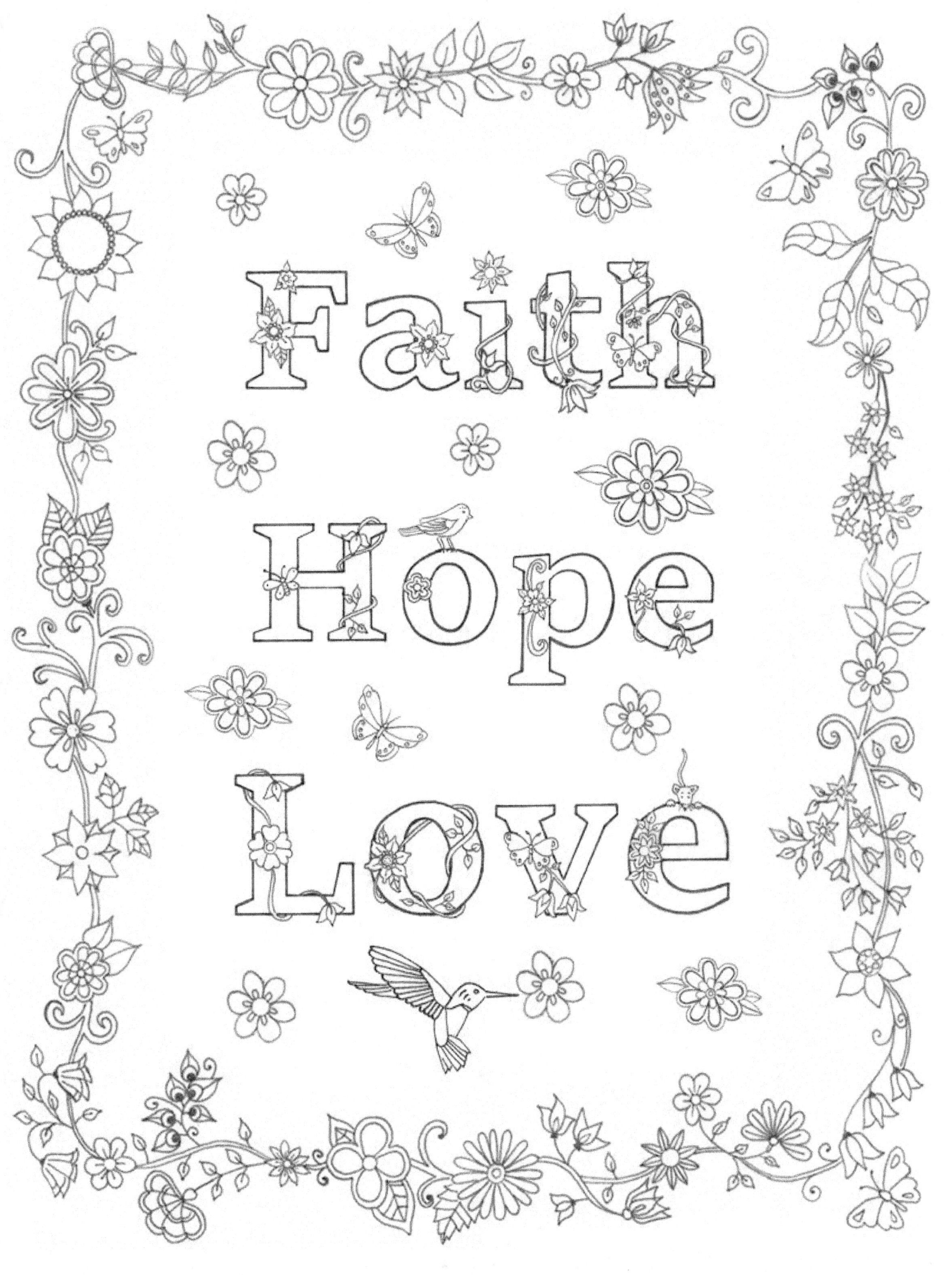

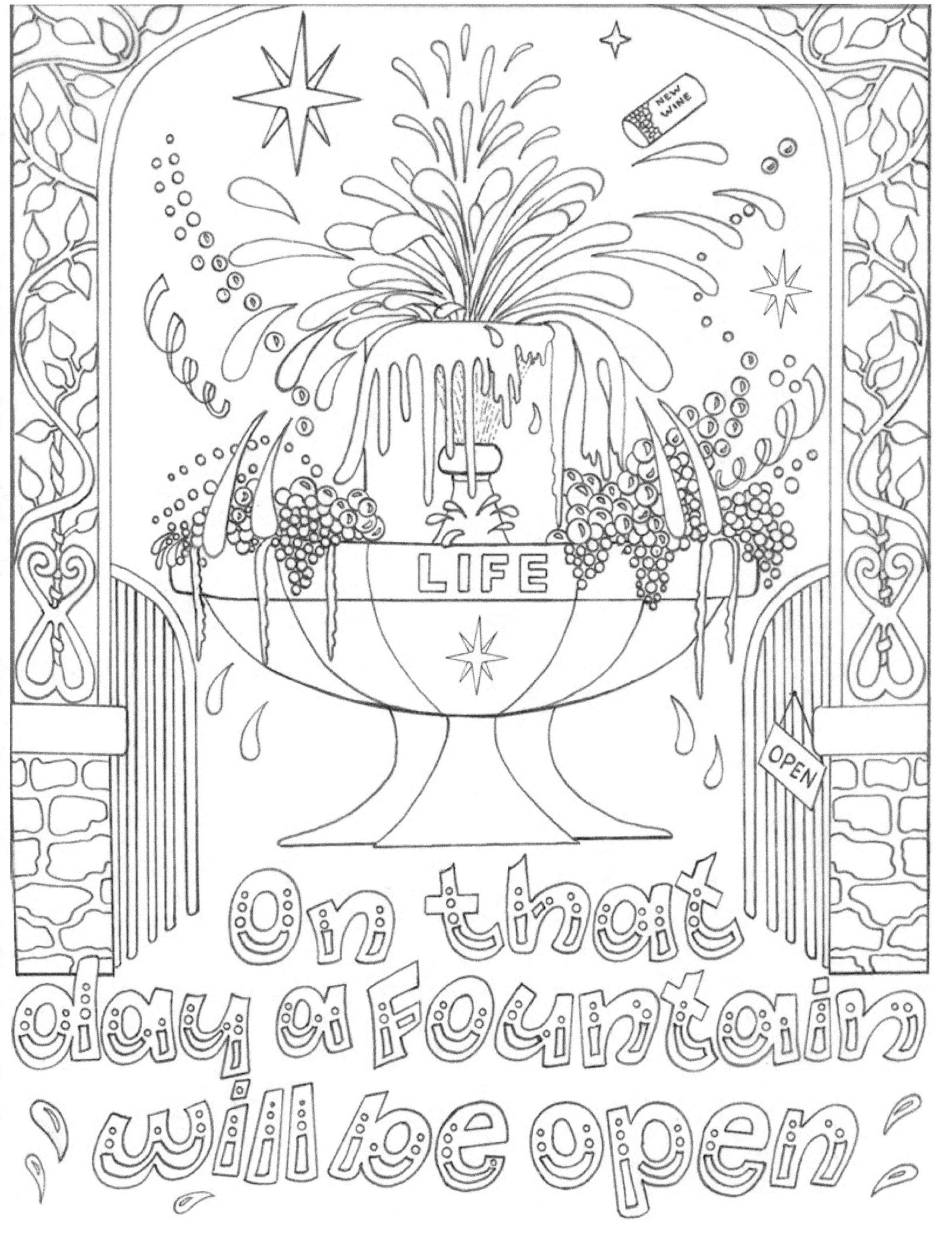

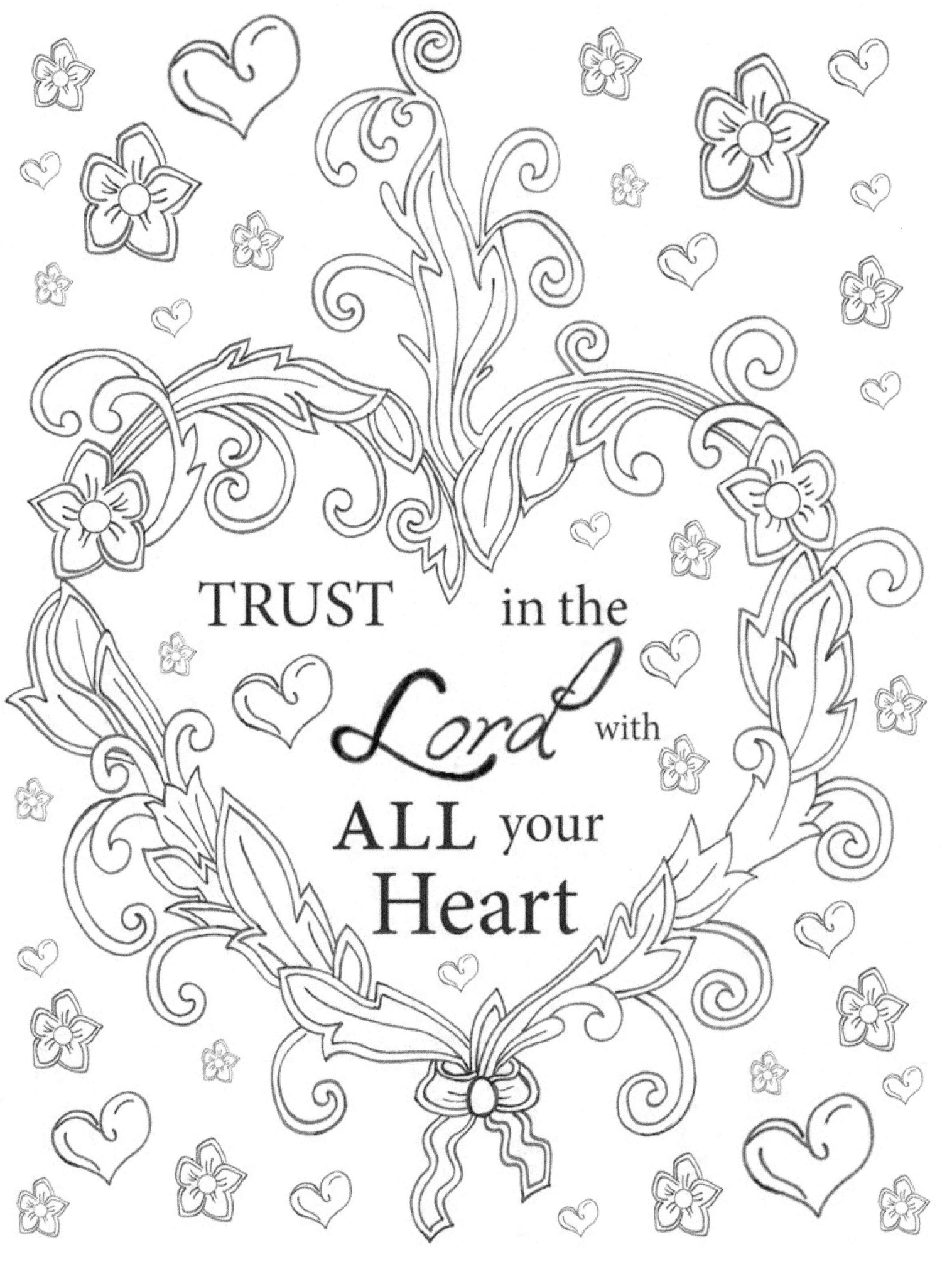

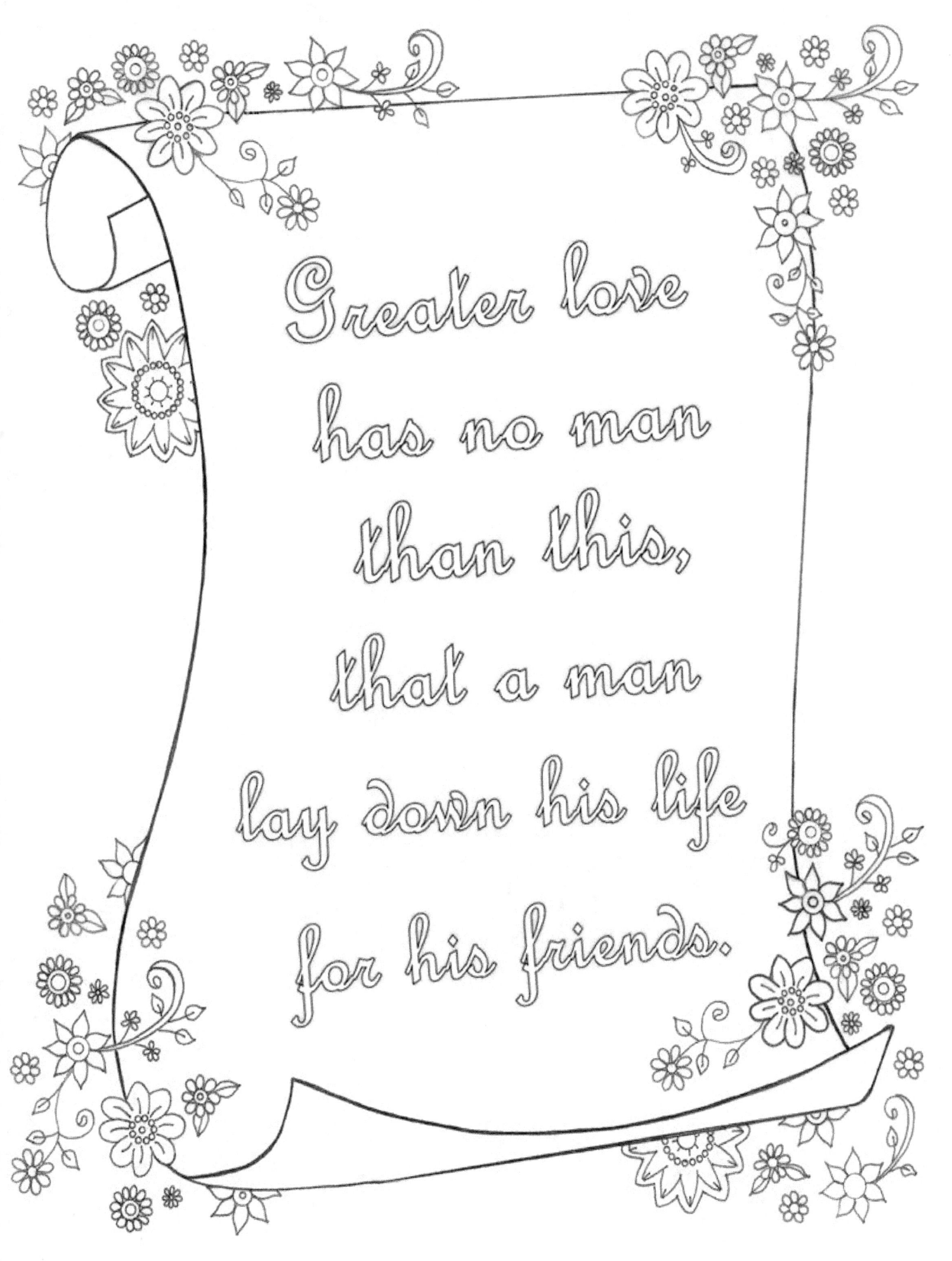

Greater love has no man than this, that a man lay down his life for his friends.

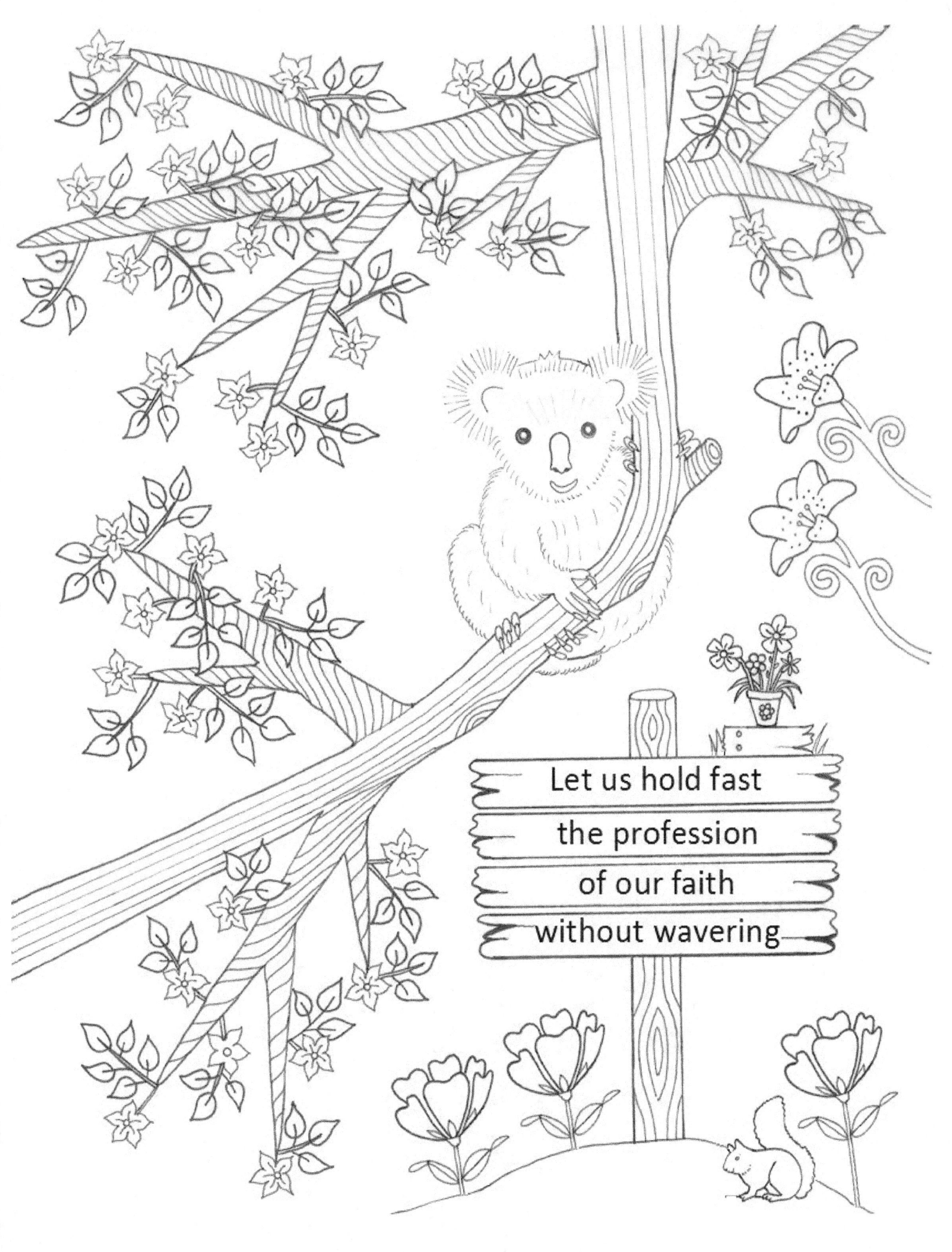

Let us hold fast
the profession
of our faith
without wavering

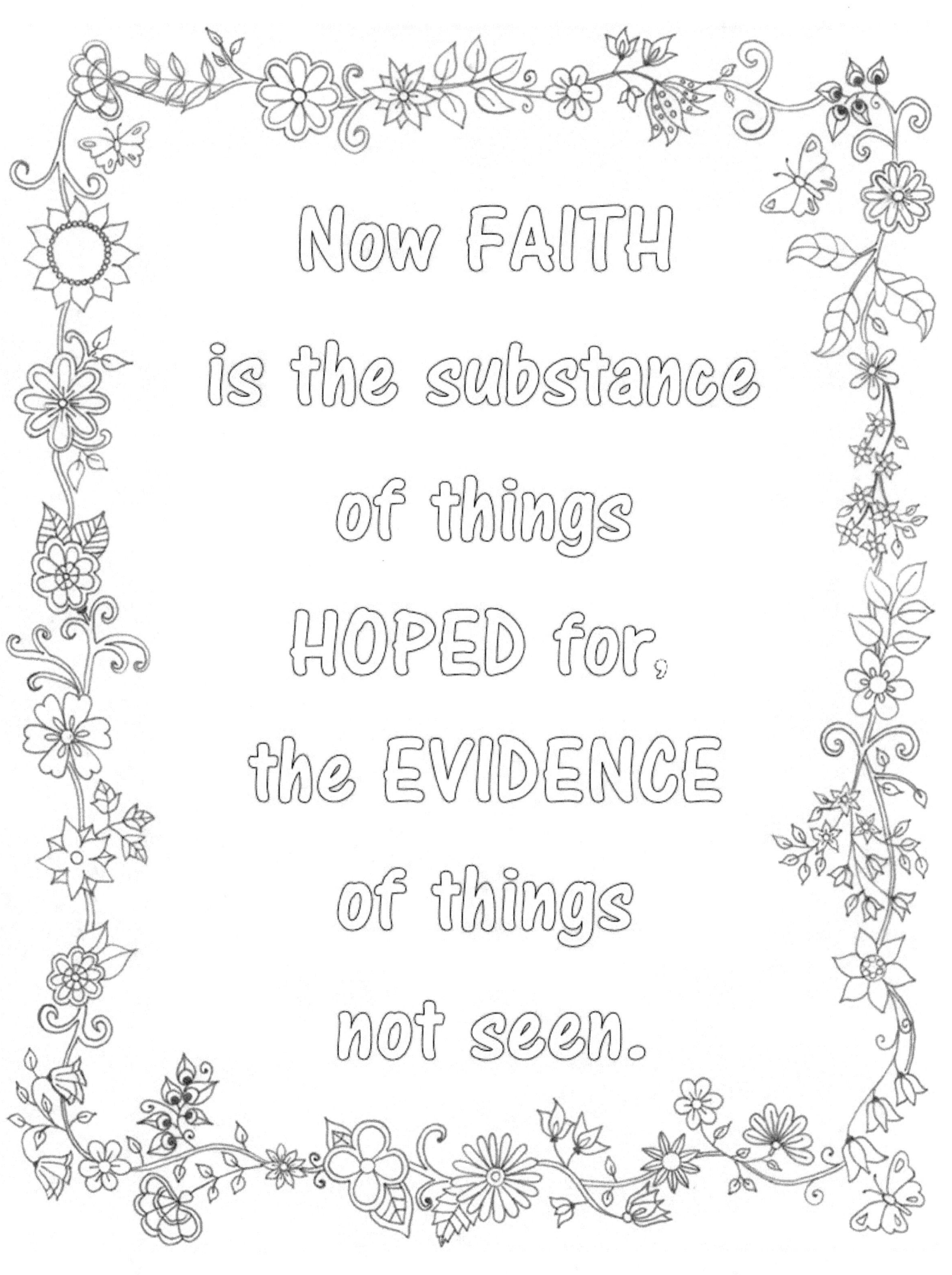

Now FAITH is the substance of things HOPED for, the EVIDENCE of things not seen.

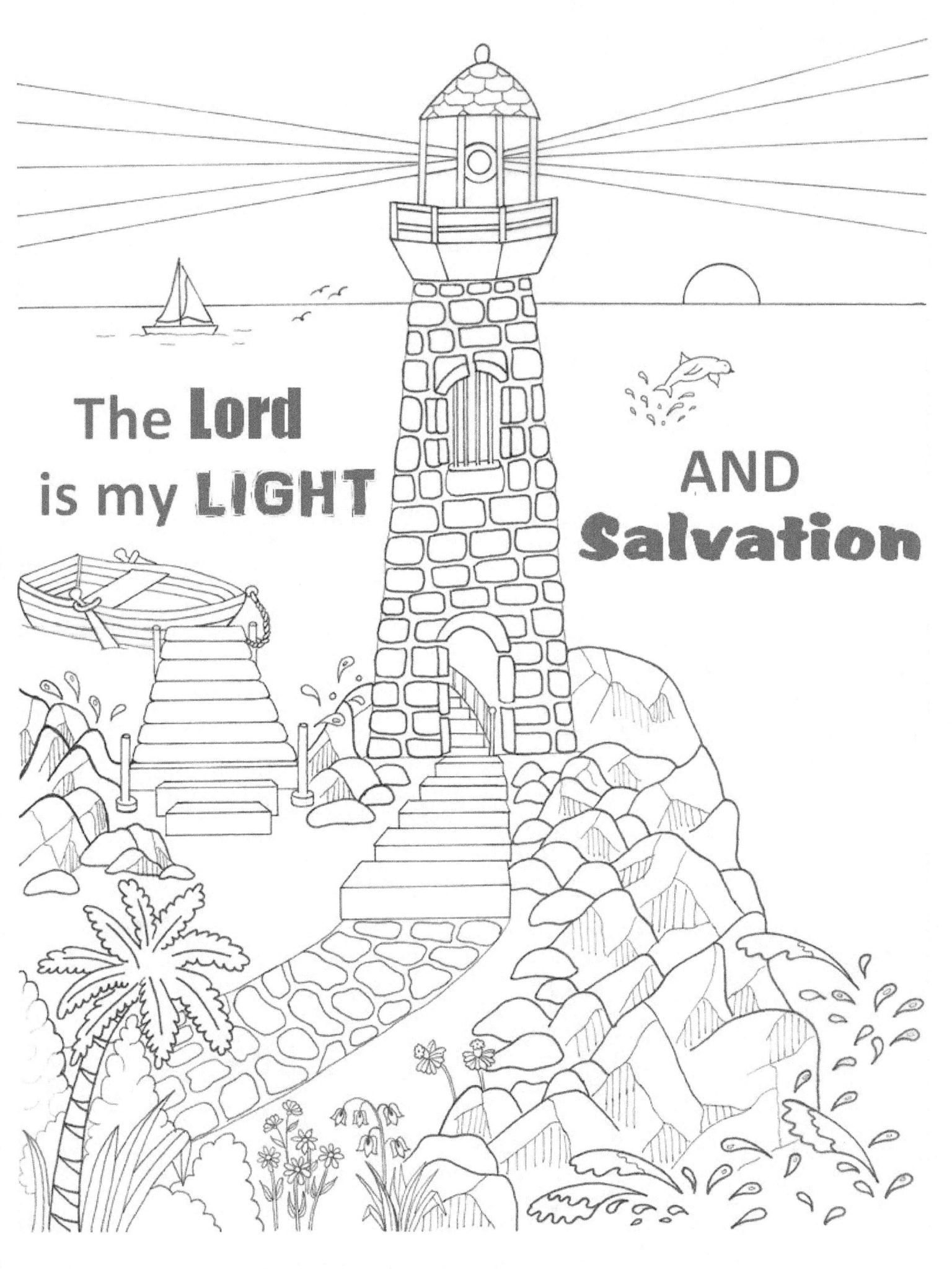

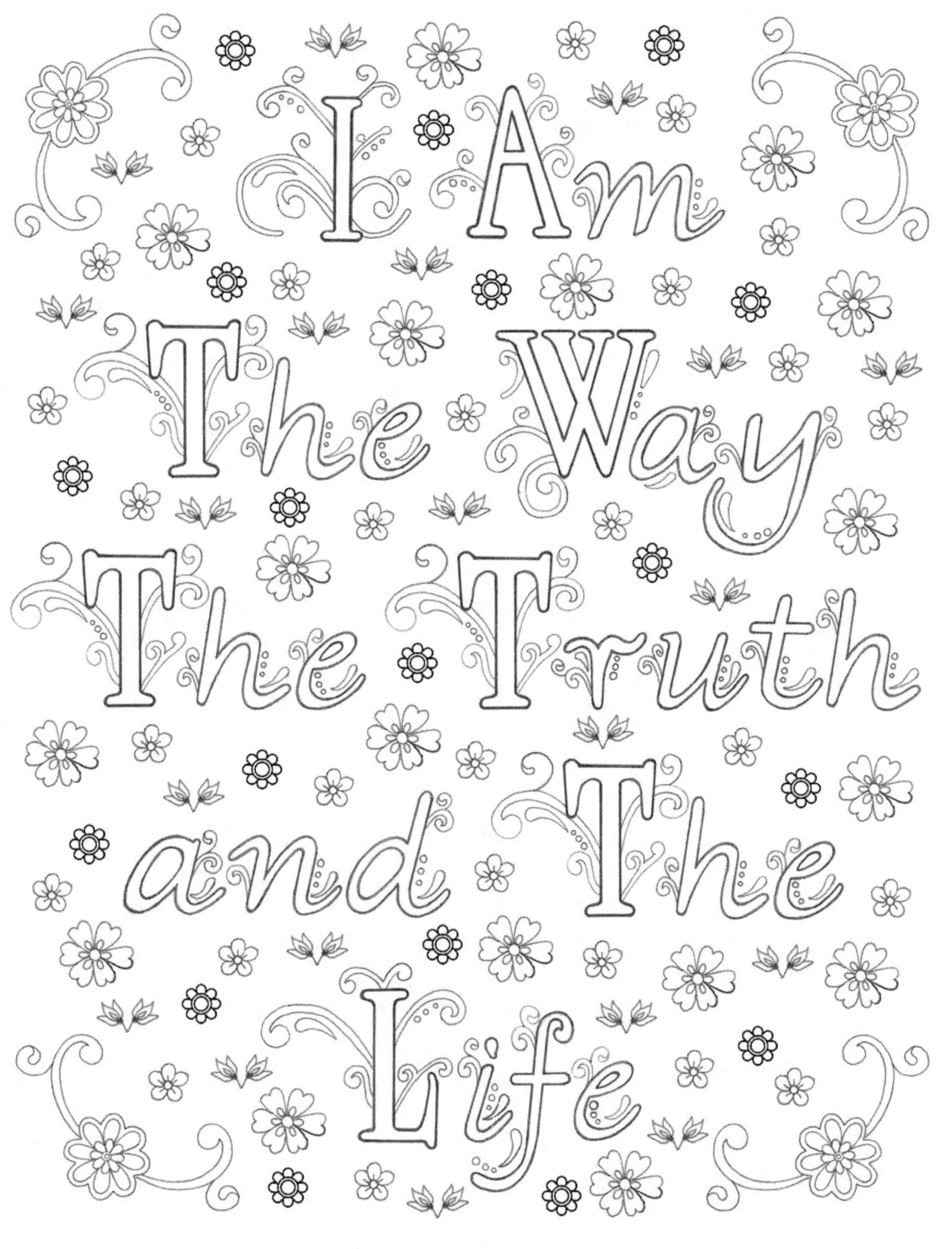

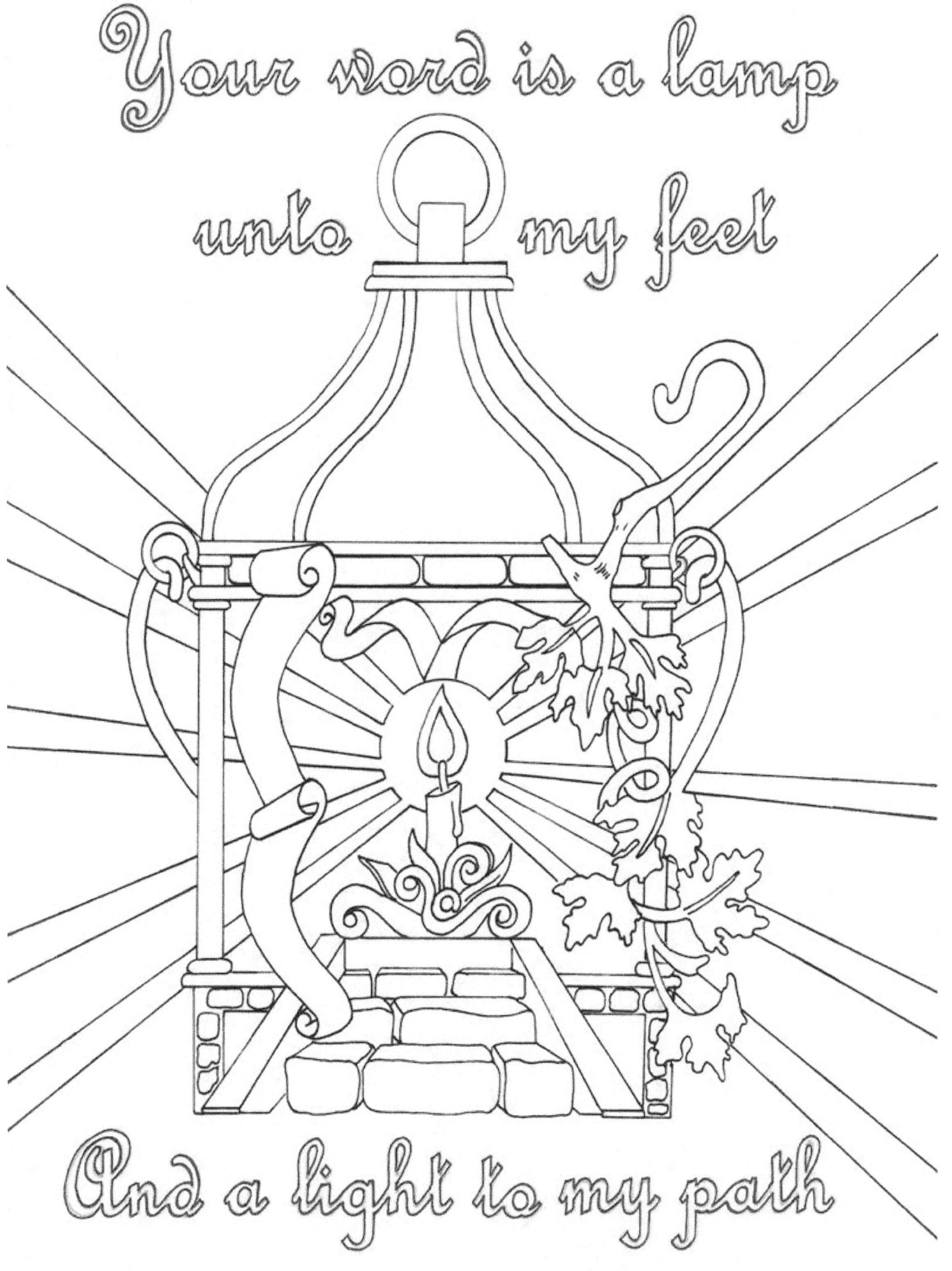

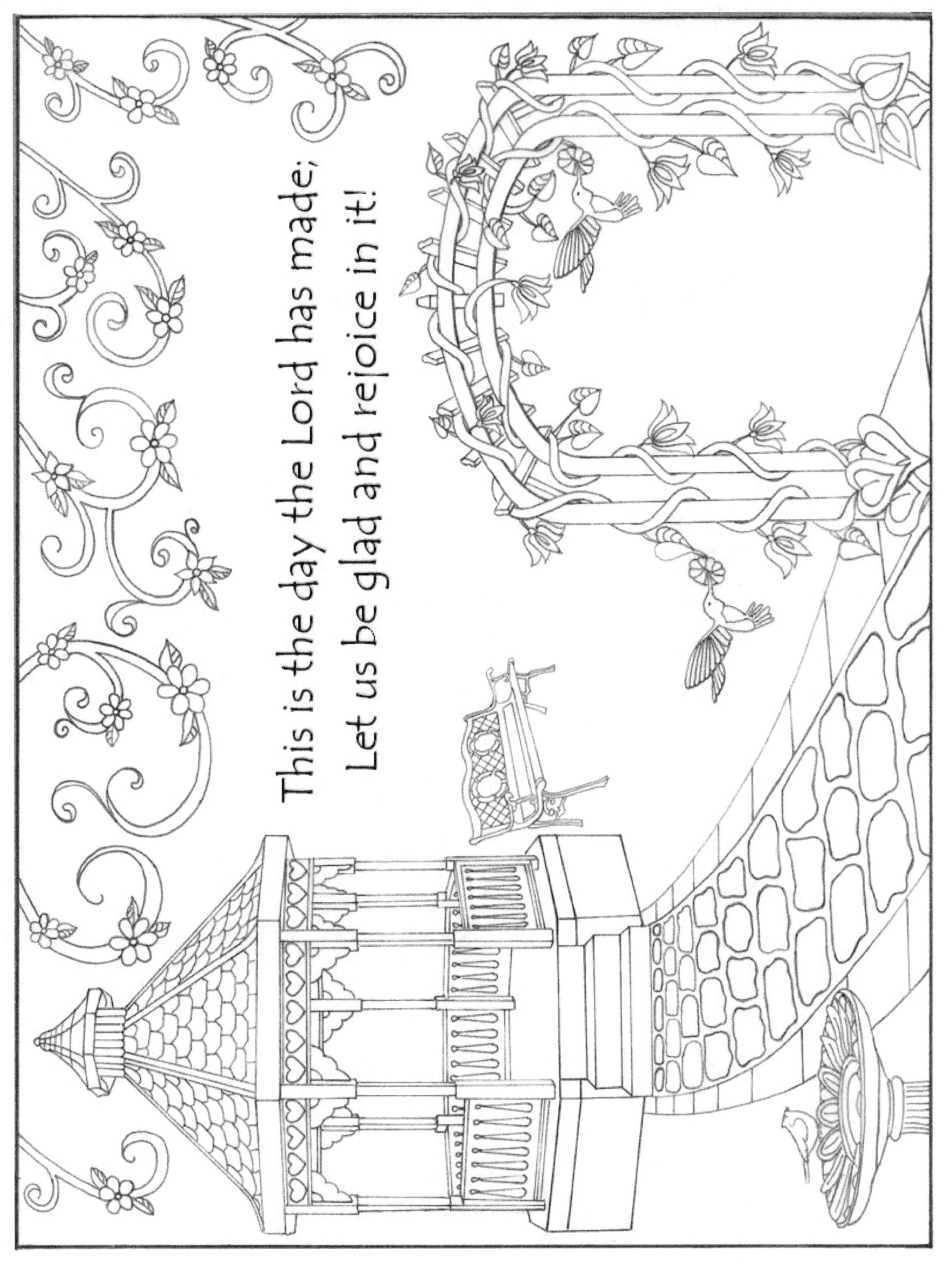

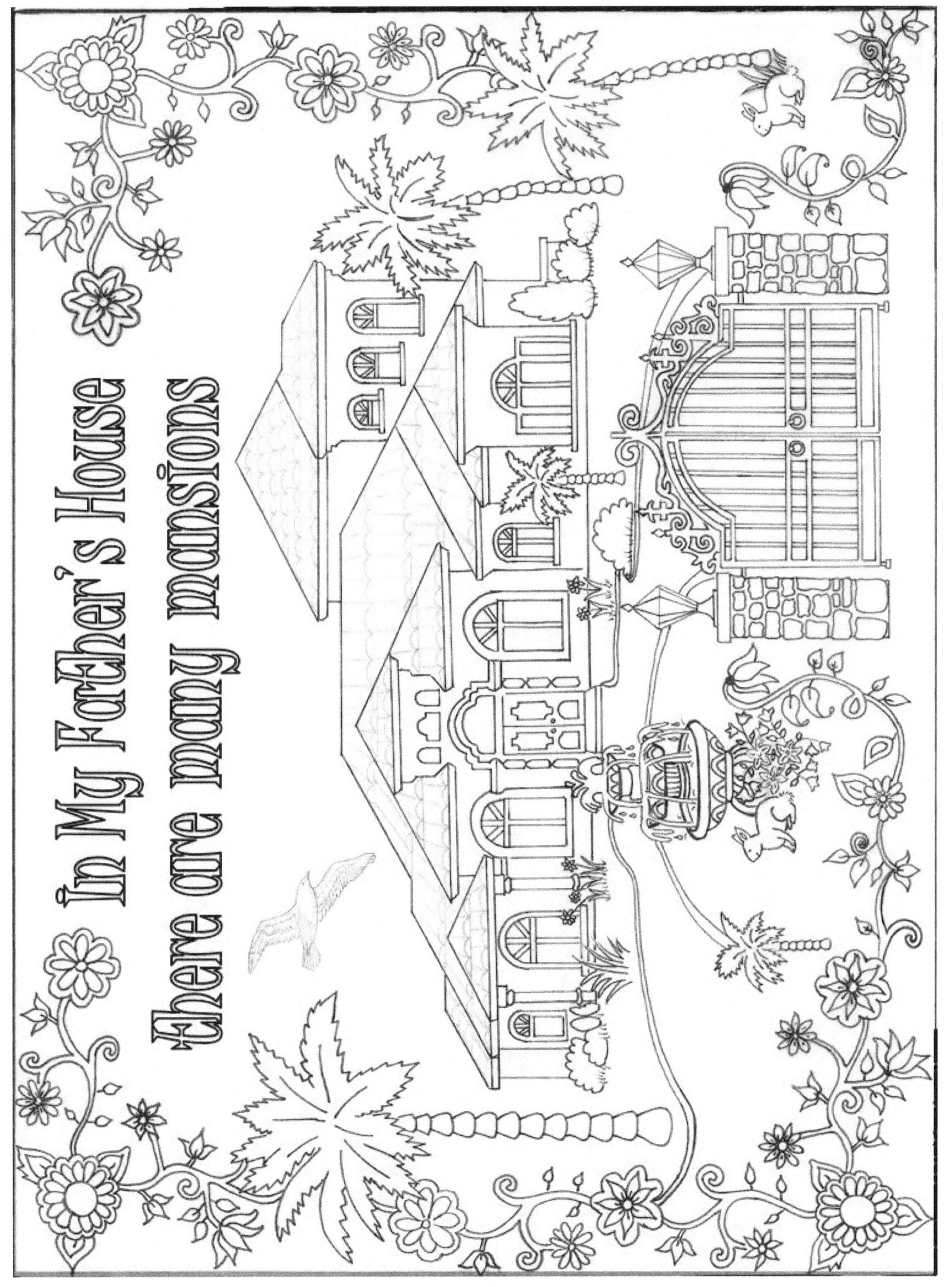

In My Father's House
There are many mansions

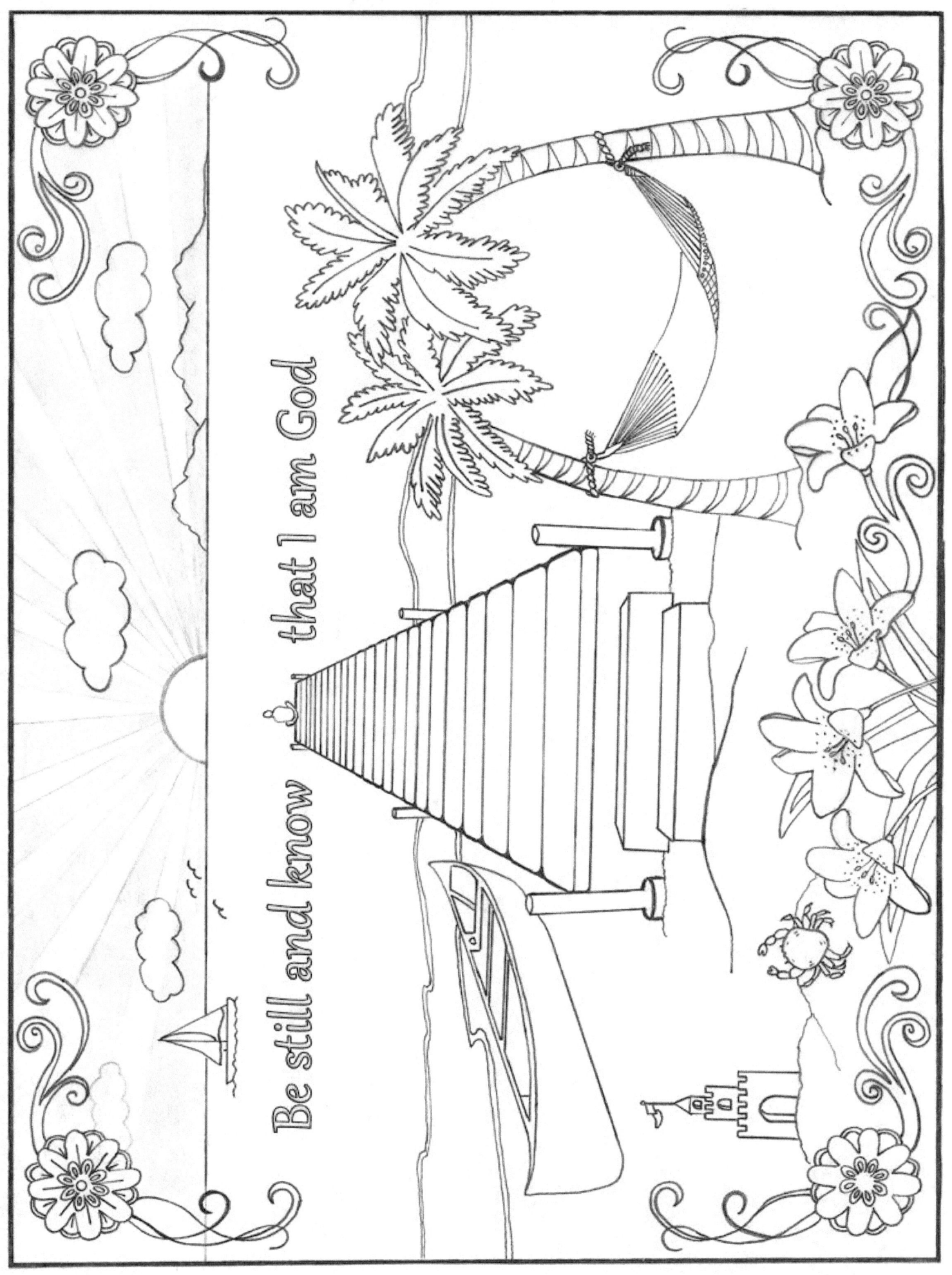

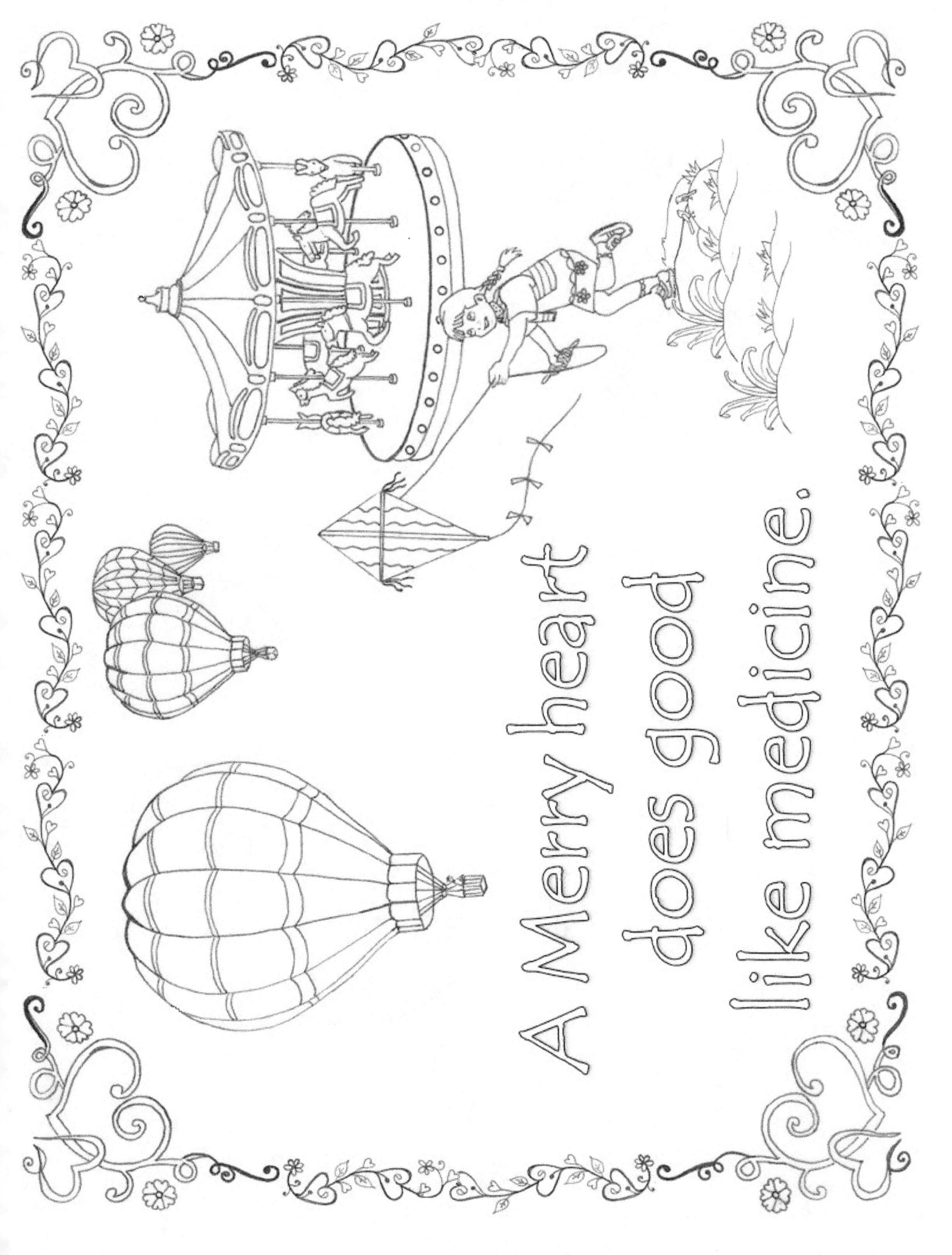

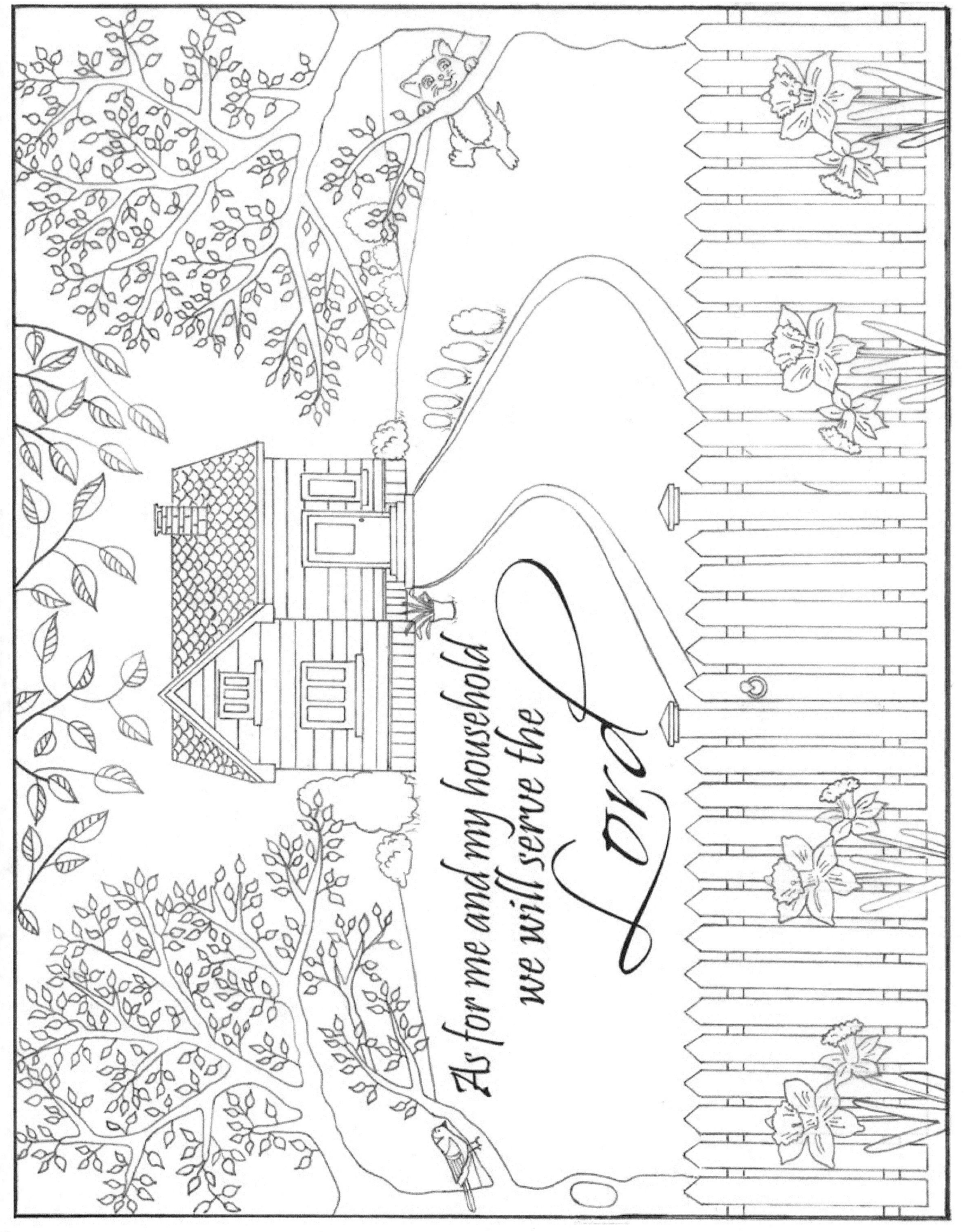

As for me and my household
we will serve the Lord

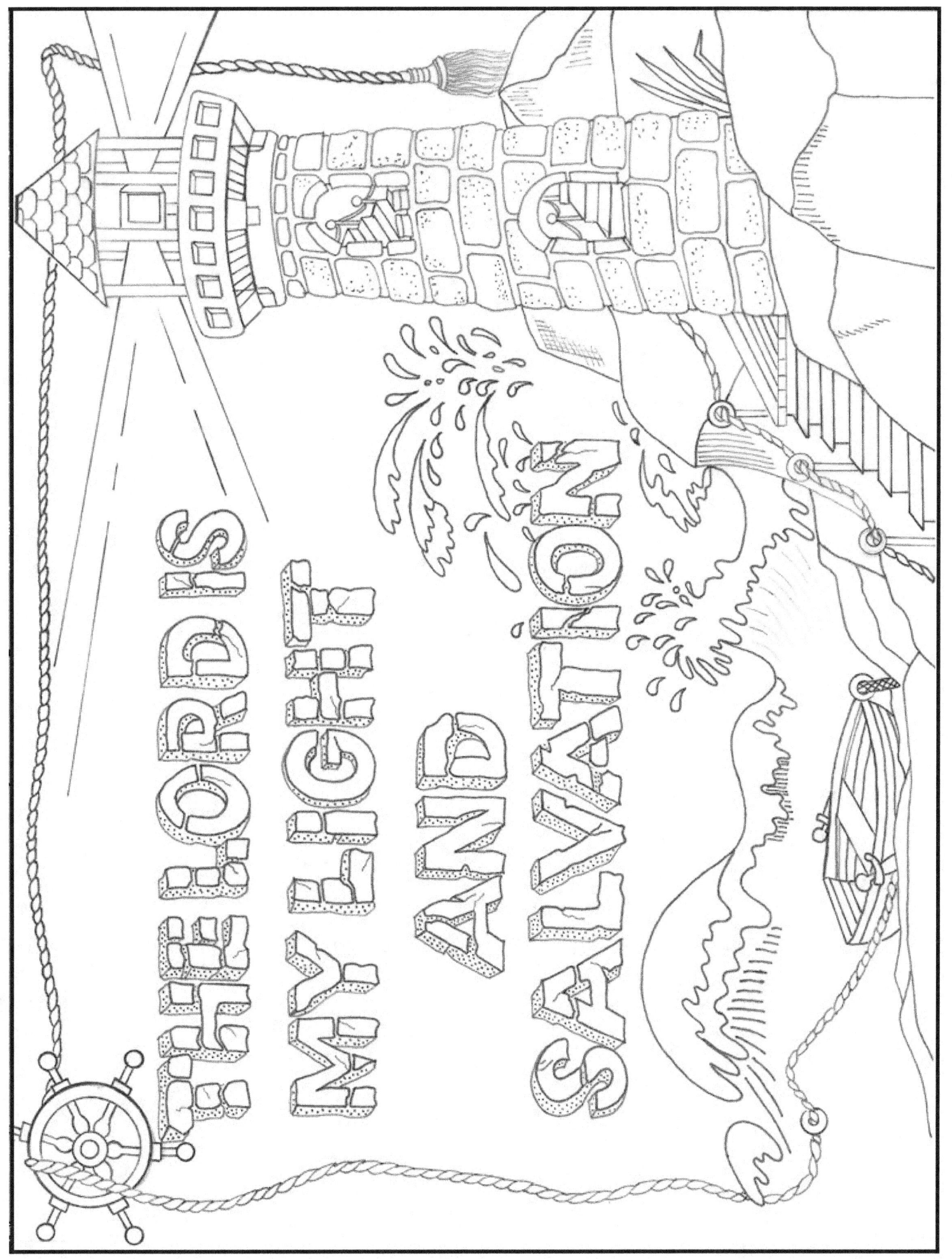

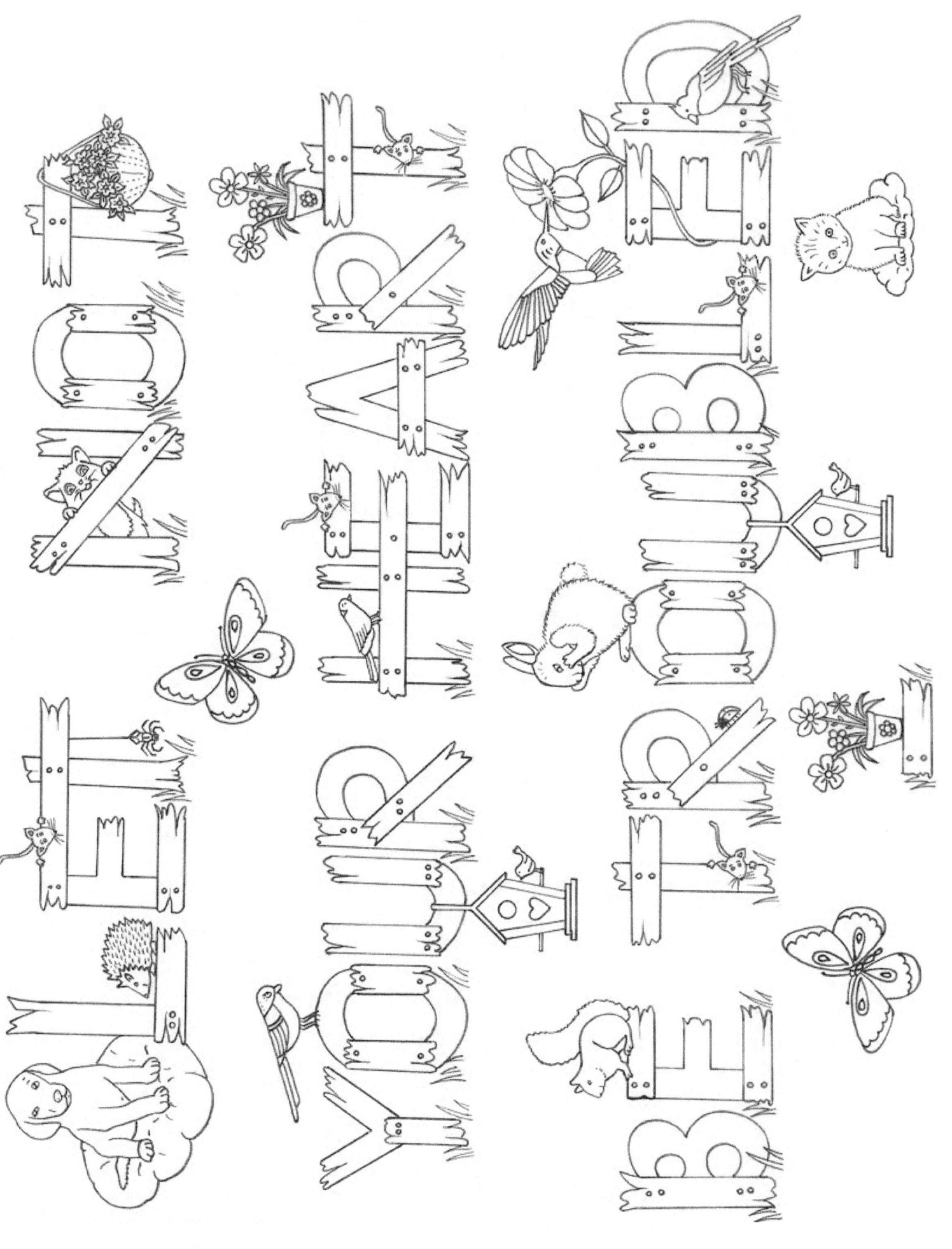

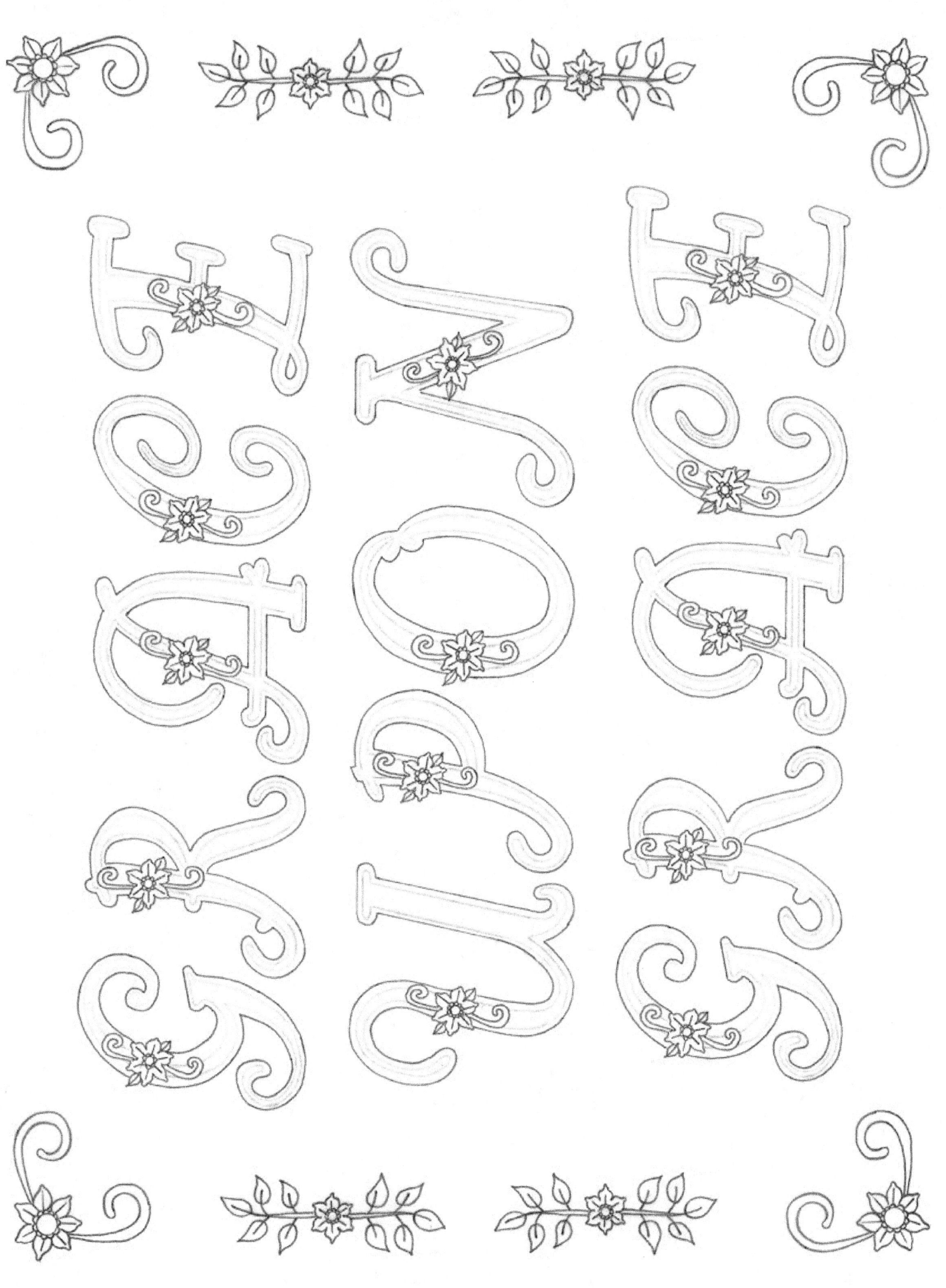

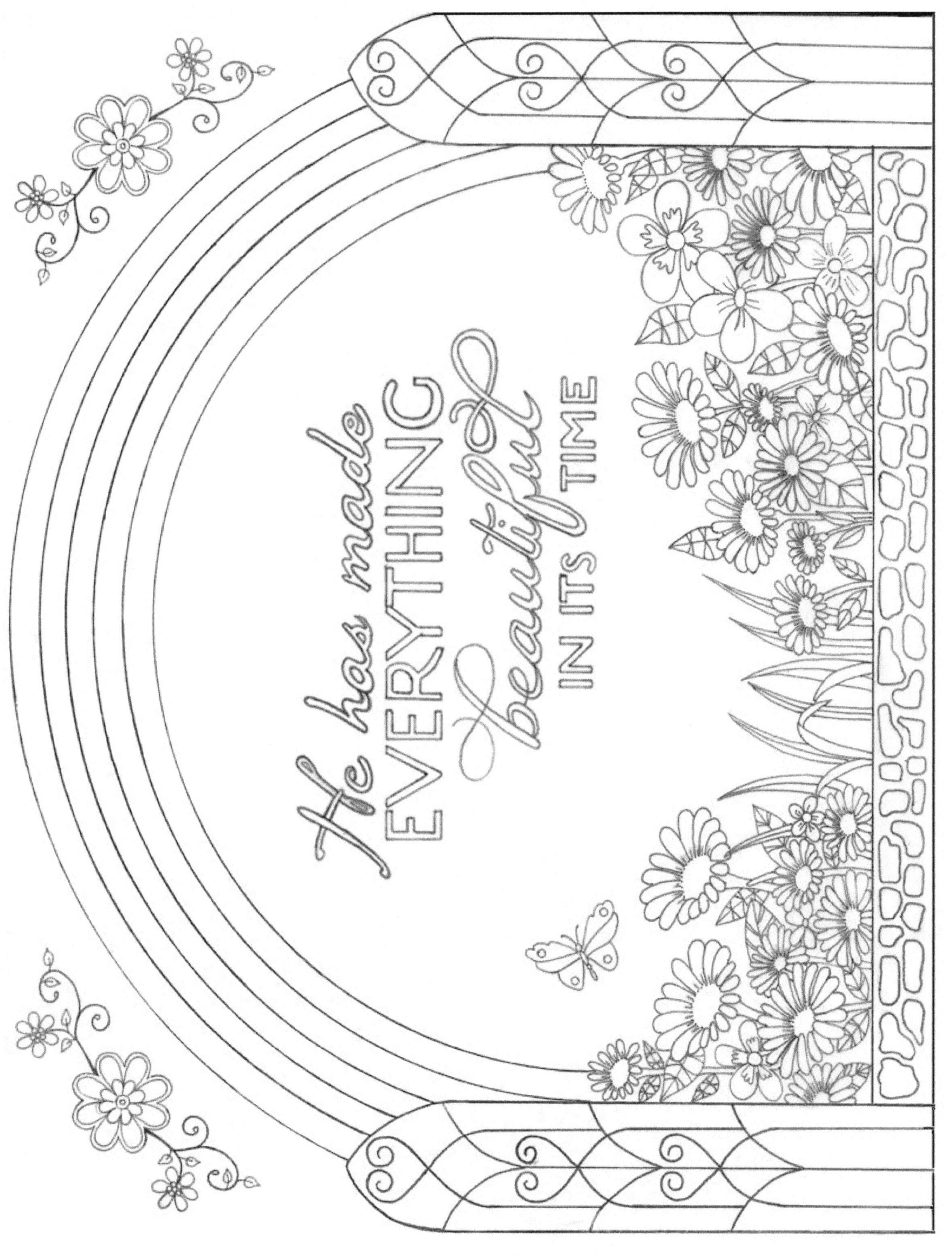

He that **Meditates** in my **LAW** day and night shall be like a **TREE** planted by the **rivers of water**, that brings forth his **Fruit** in his season

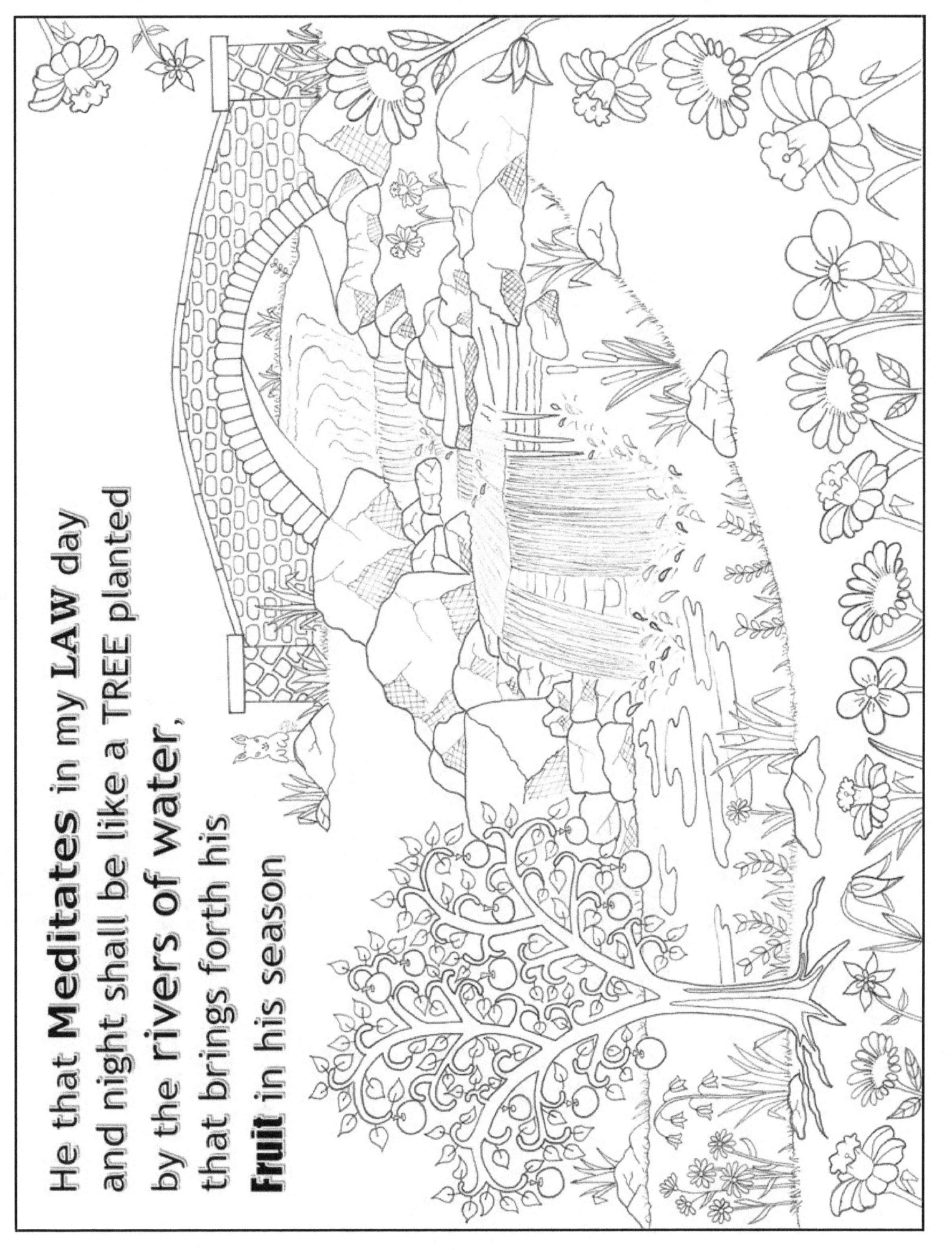

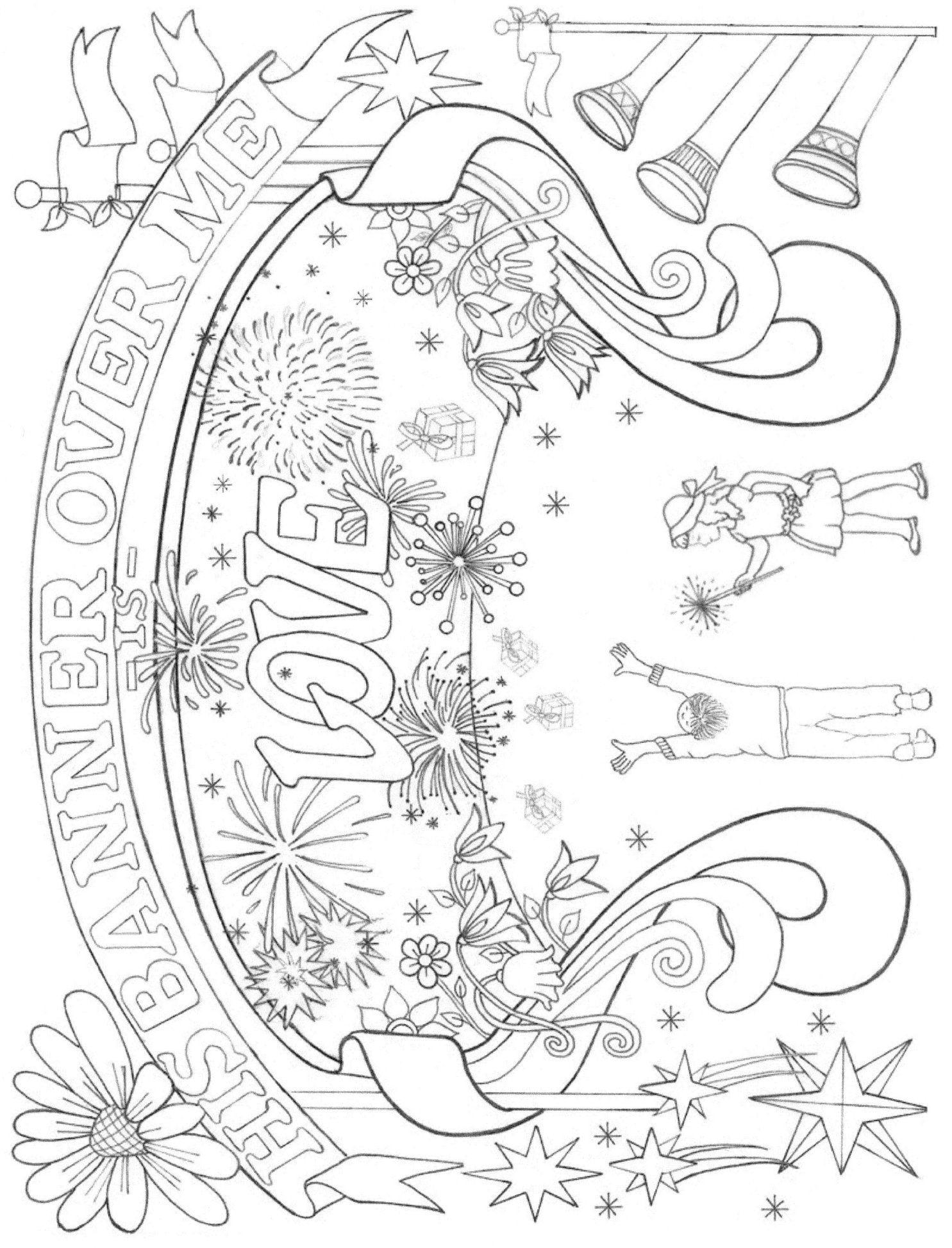

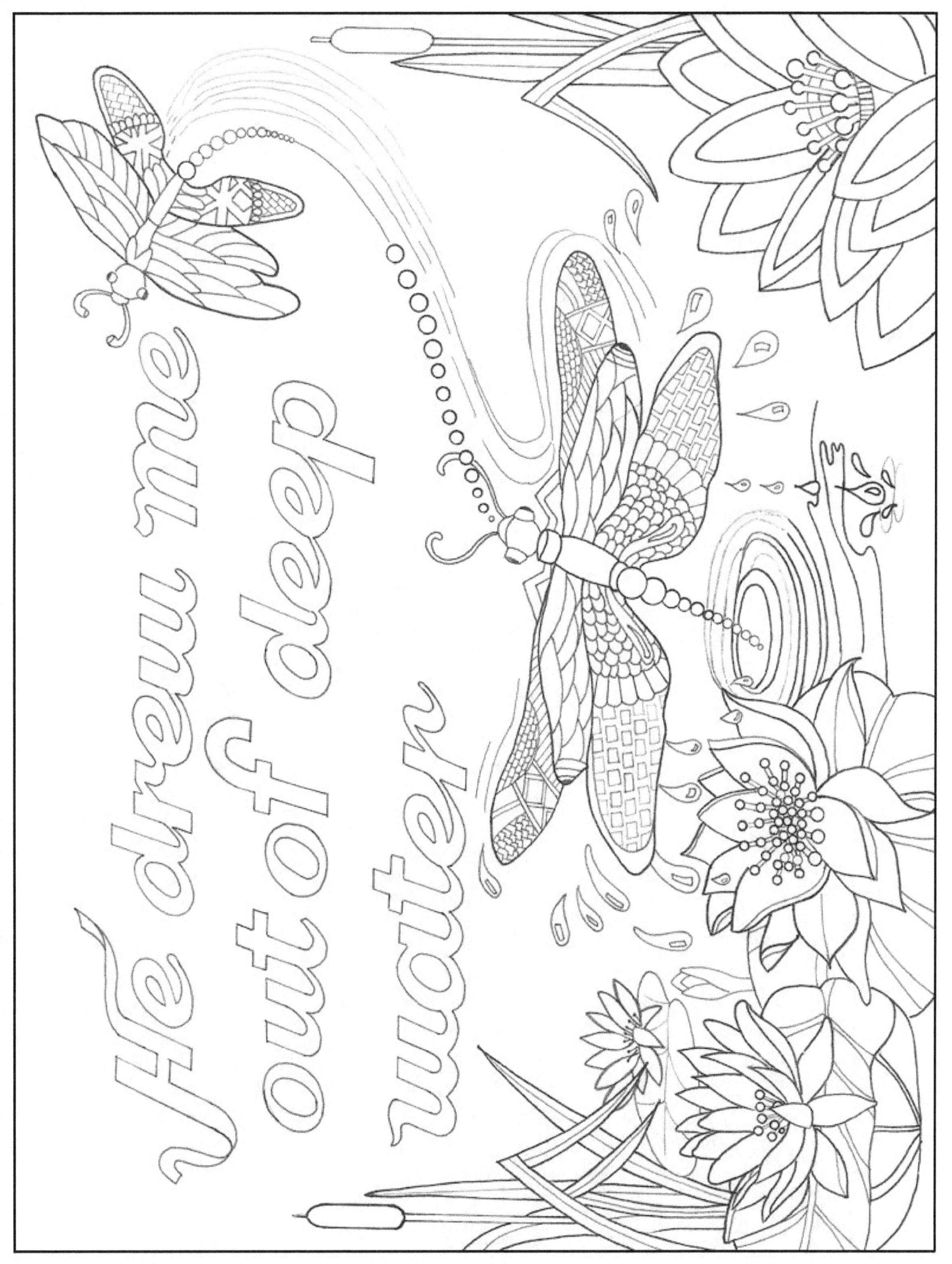

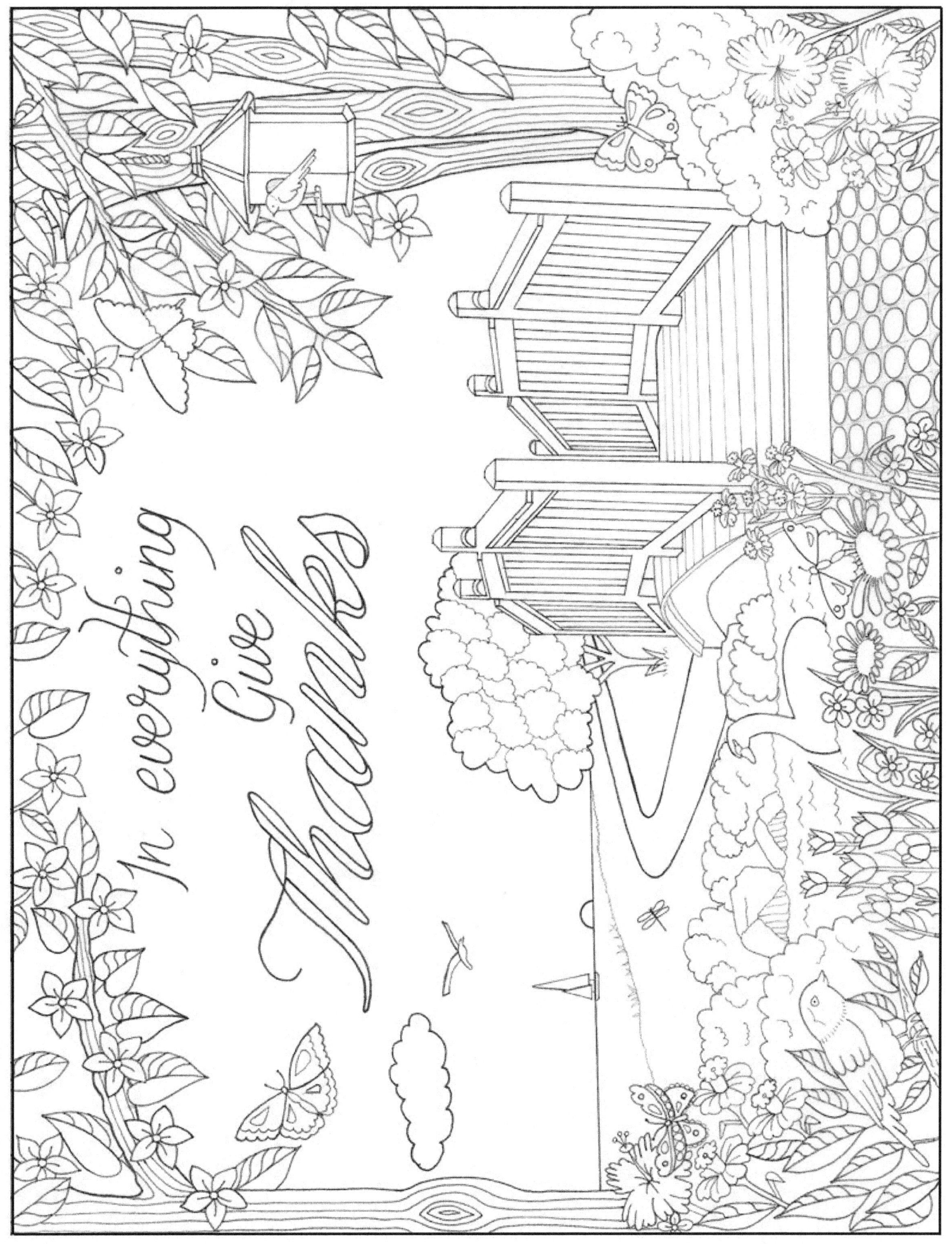

My soul doth magnify the Lord. and my spirit hath rejoiced in God my Saviour.

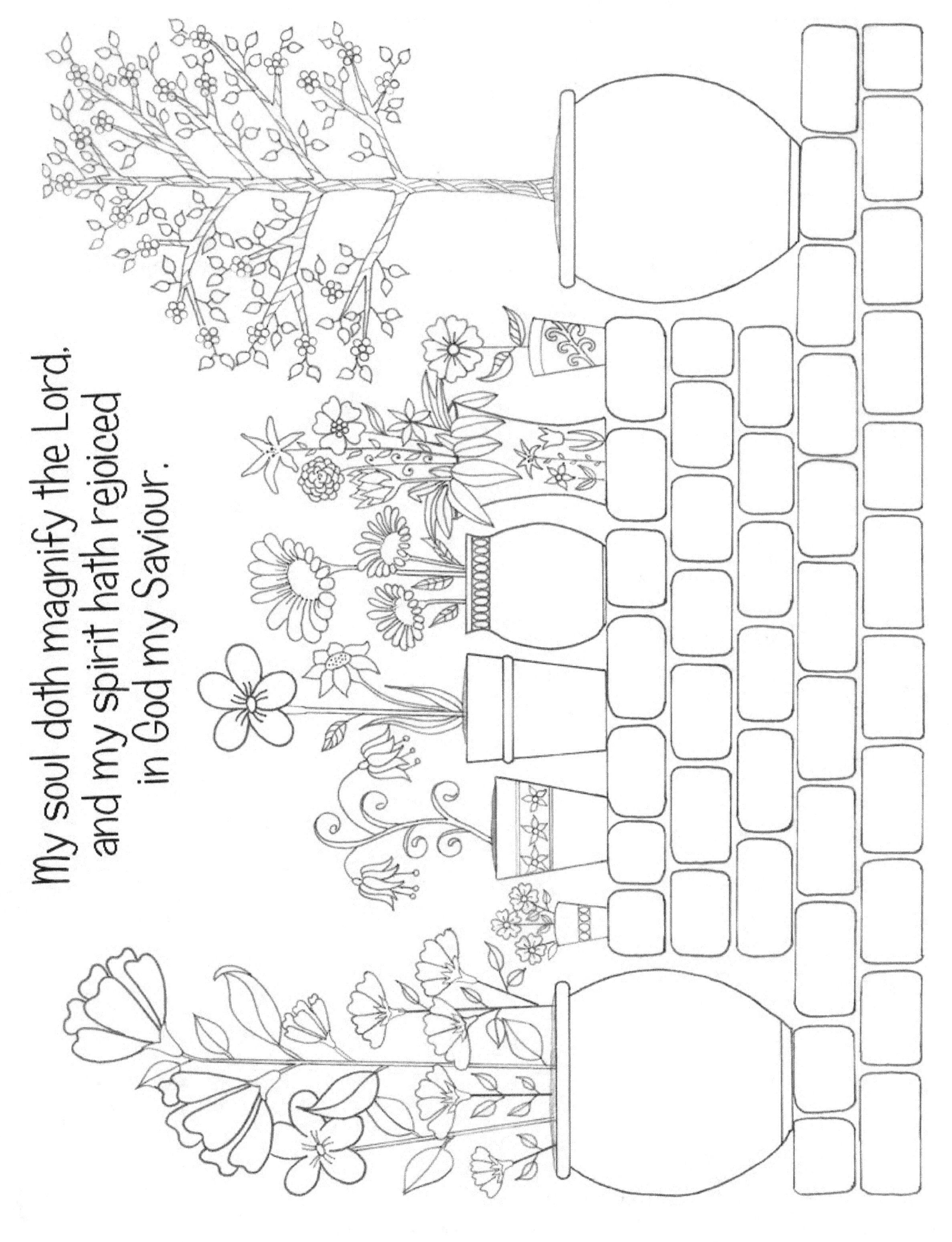

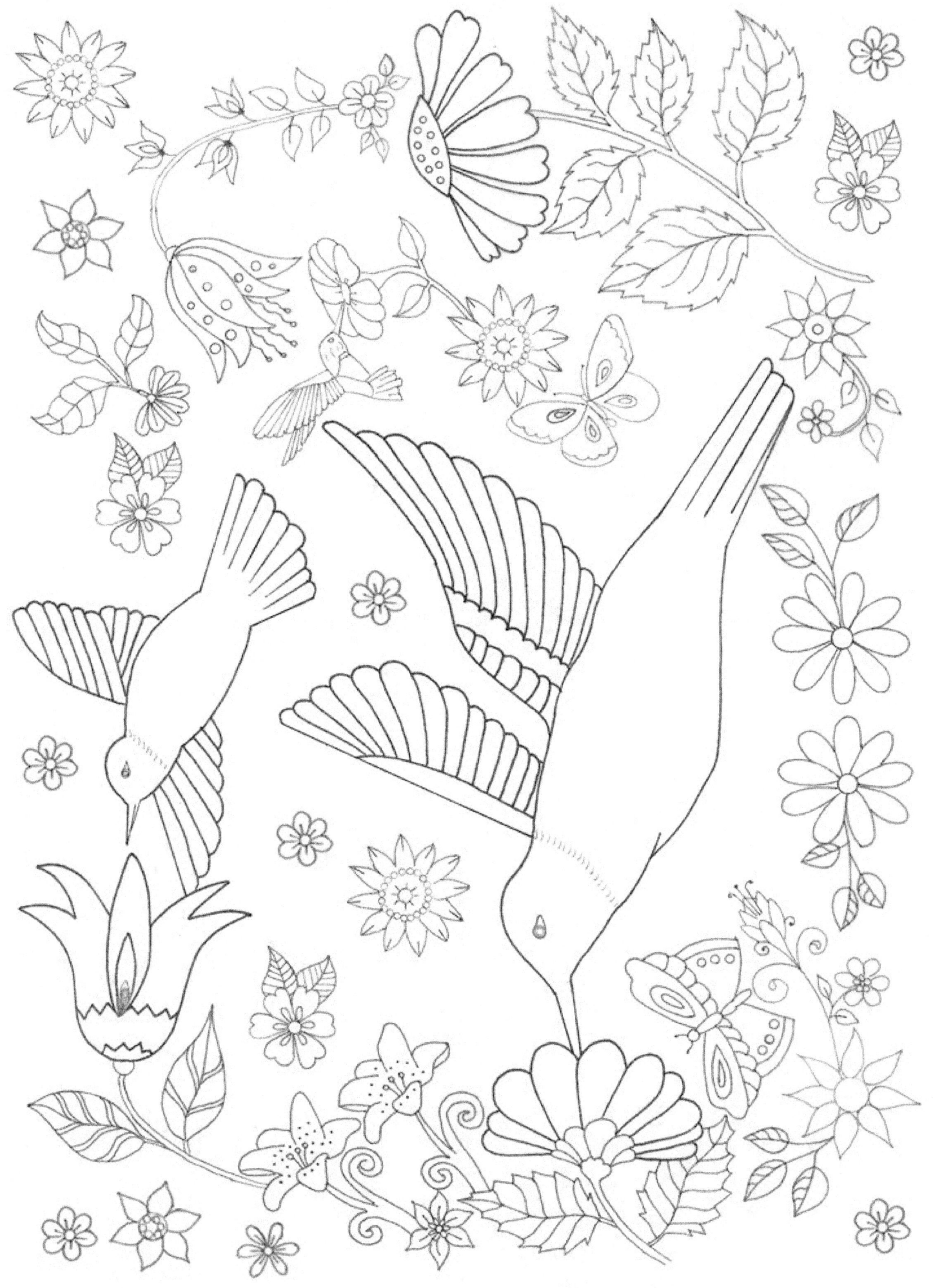

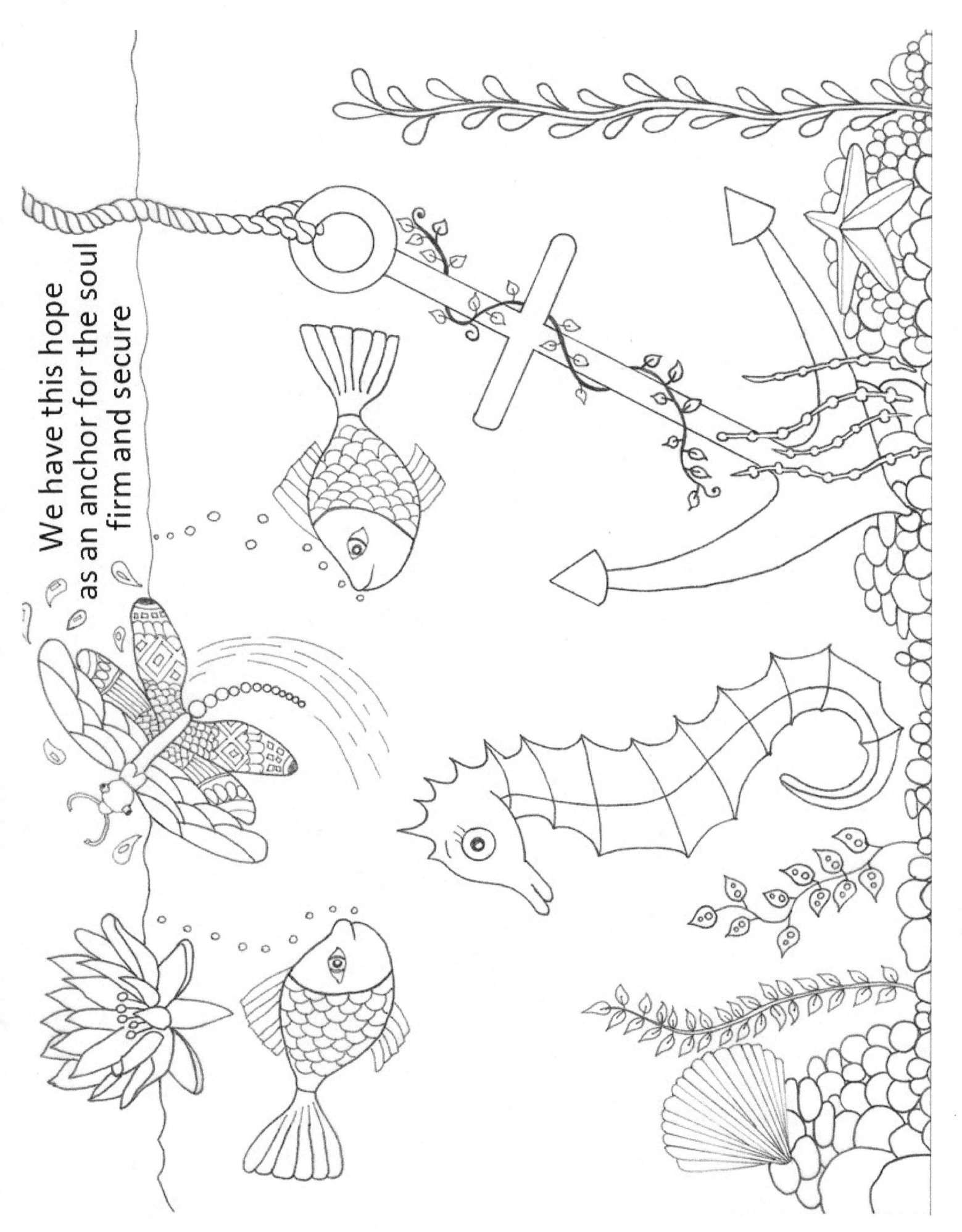

We have this hope as an anchor for the soul firm and secure

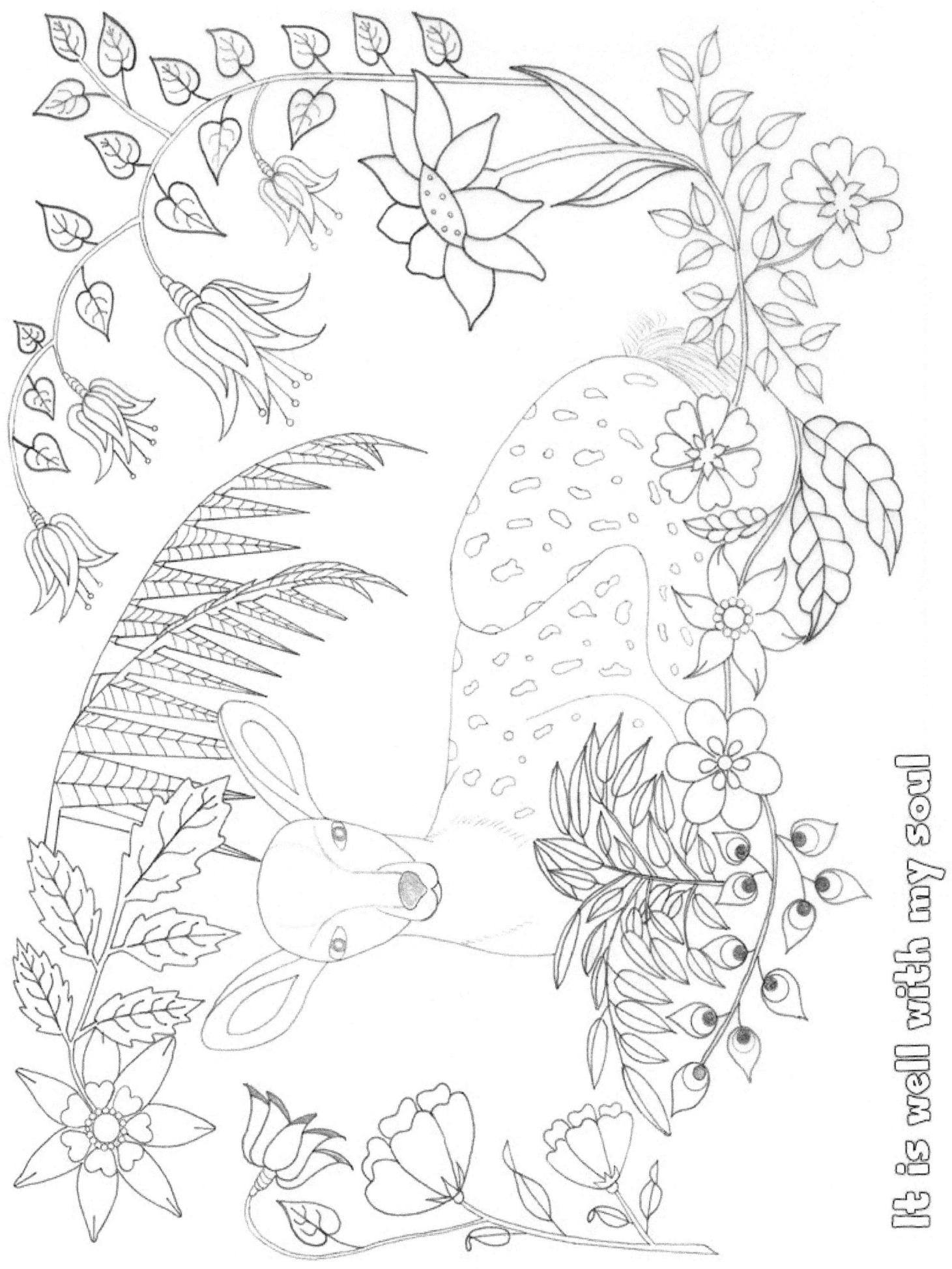

It is well with my soul

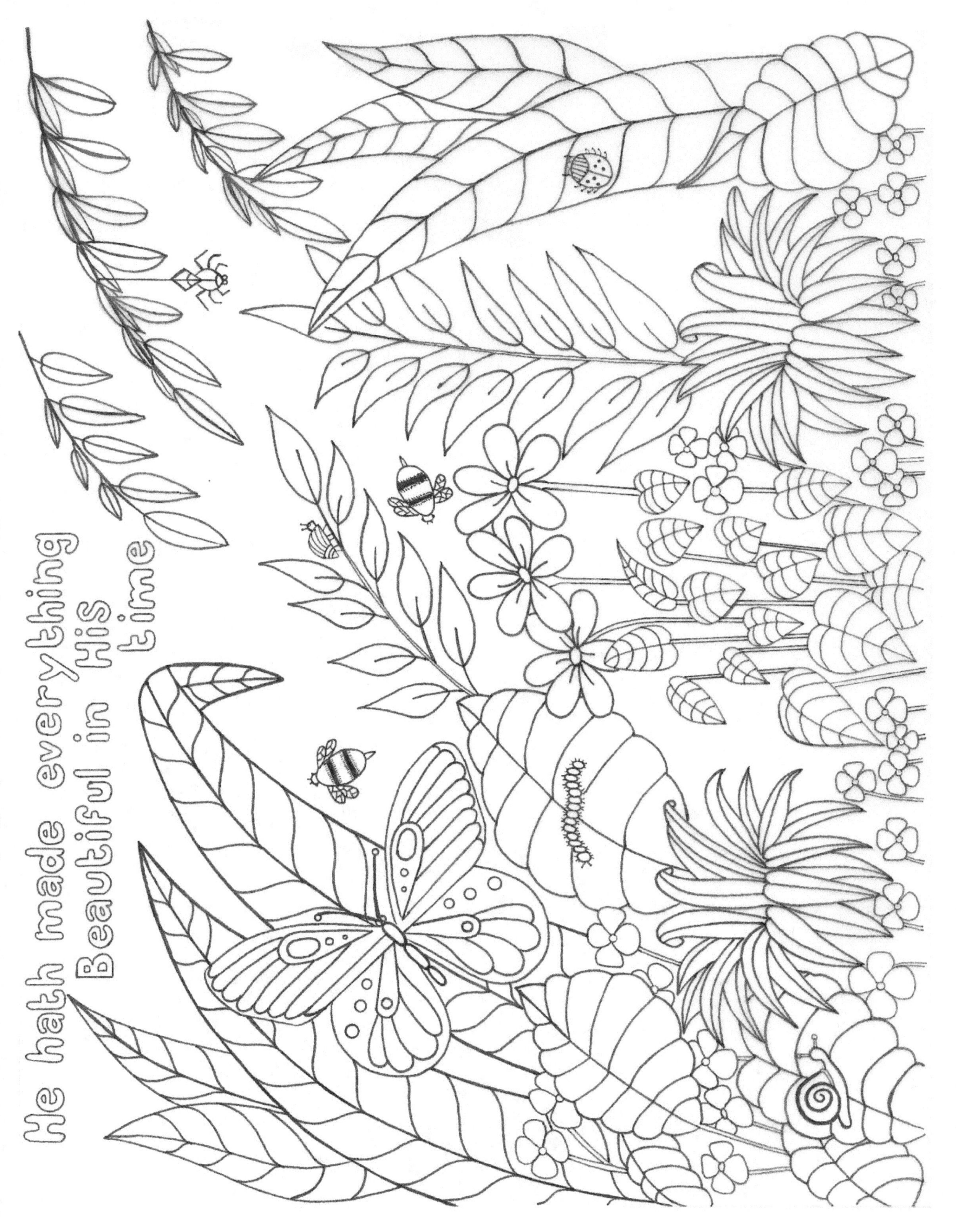

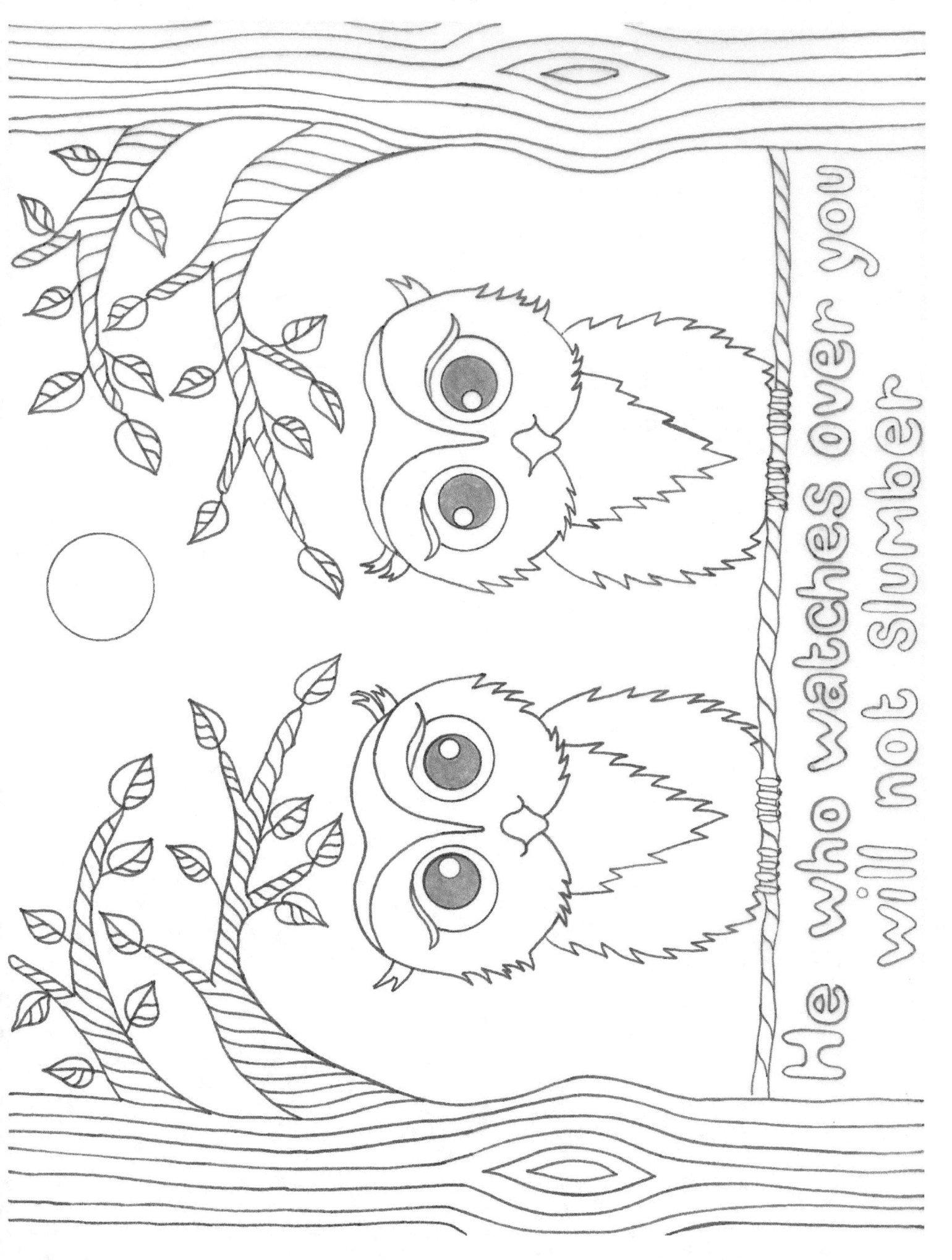

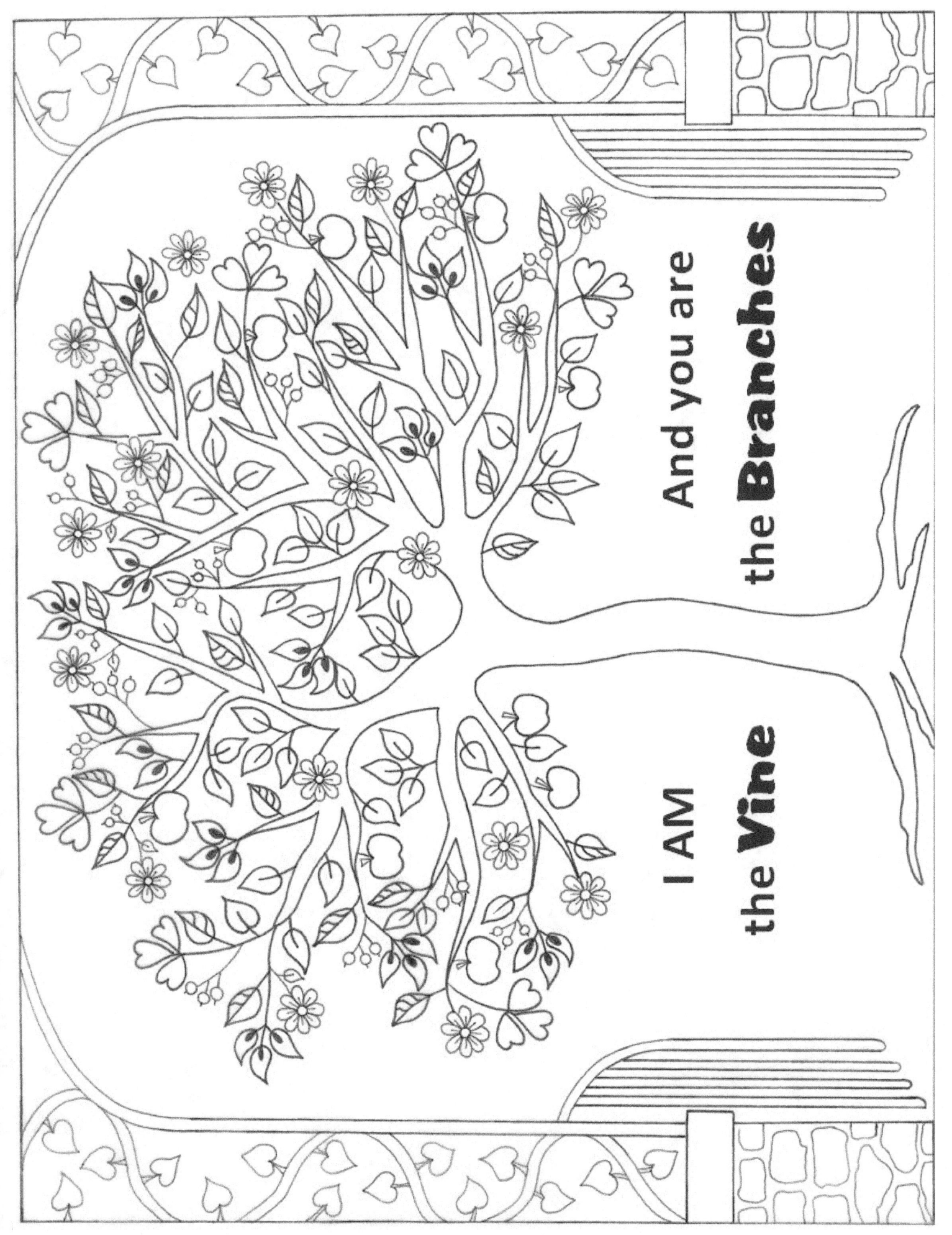

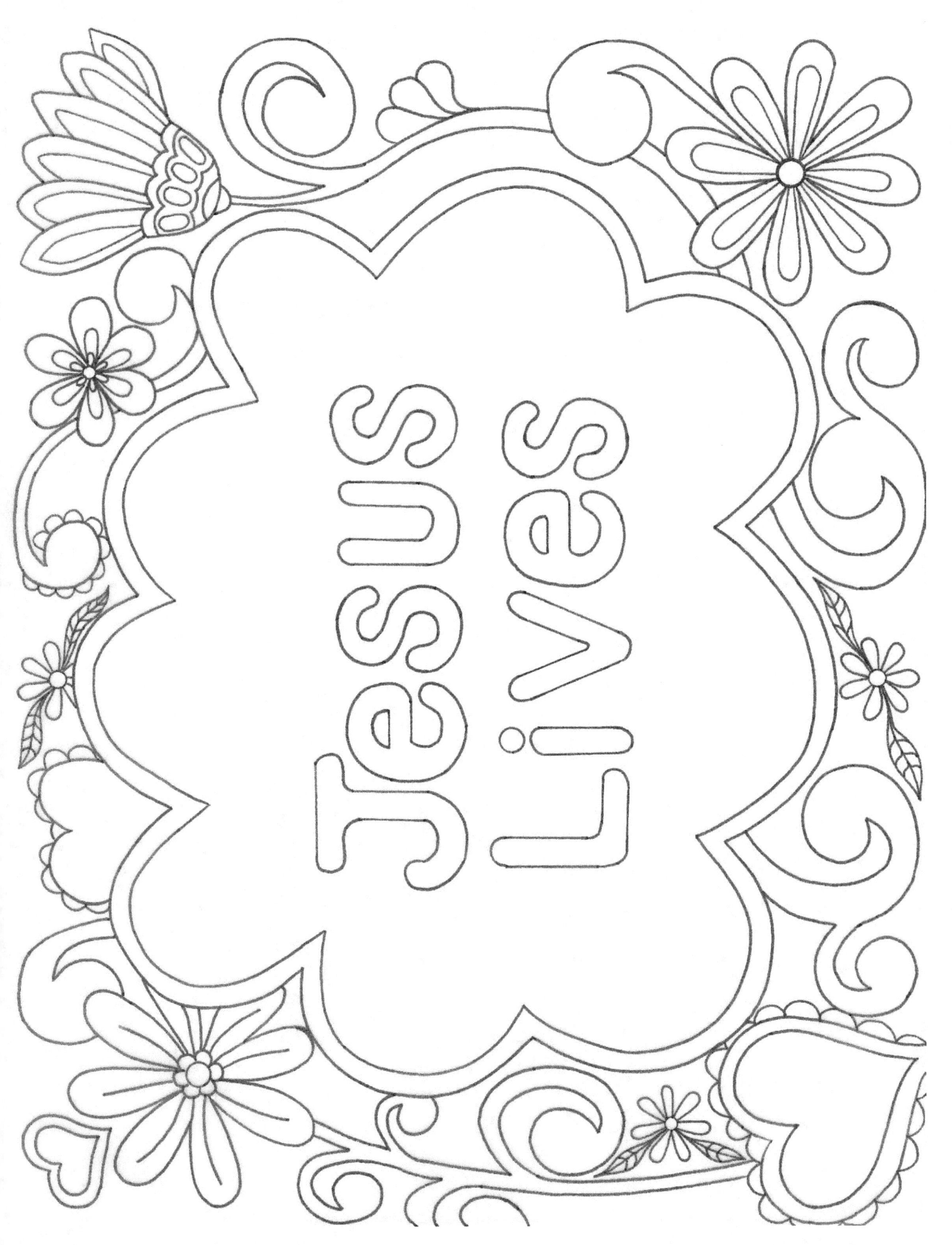

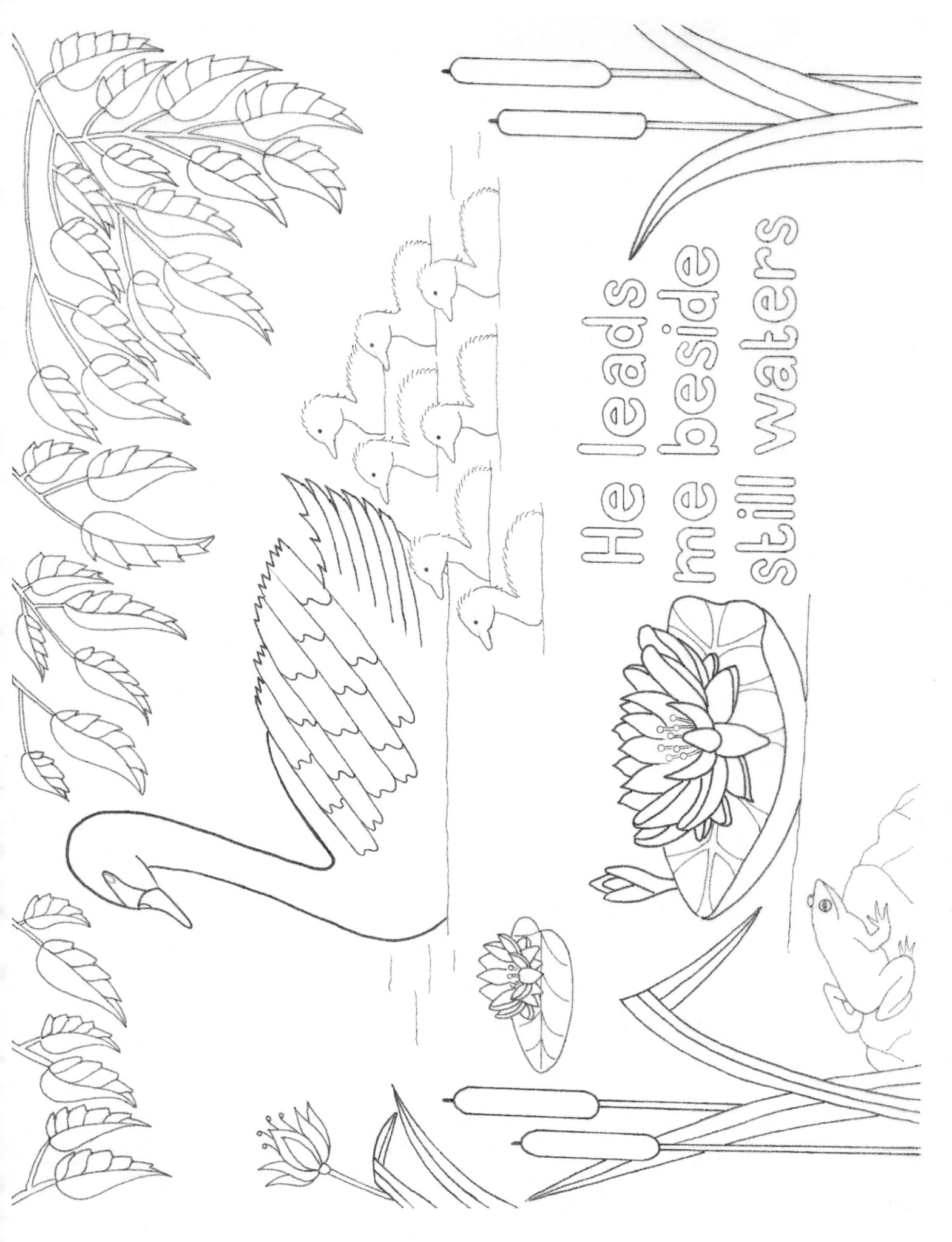

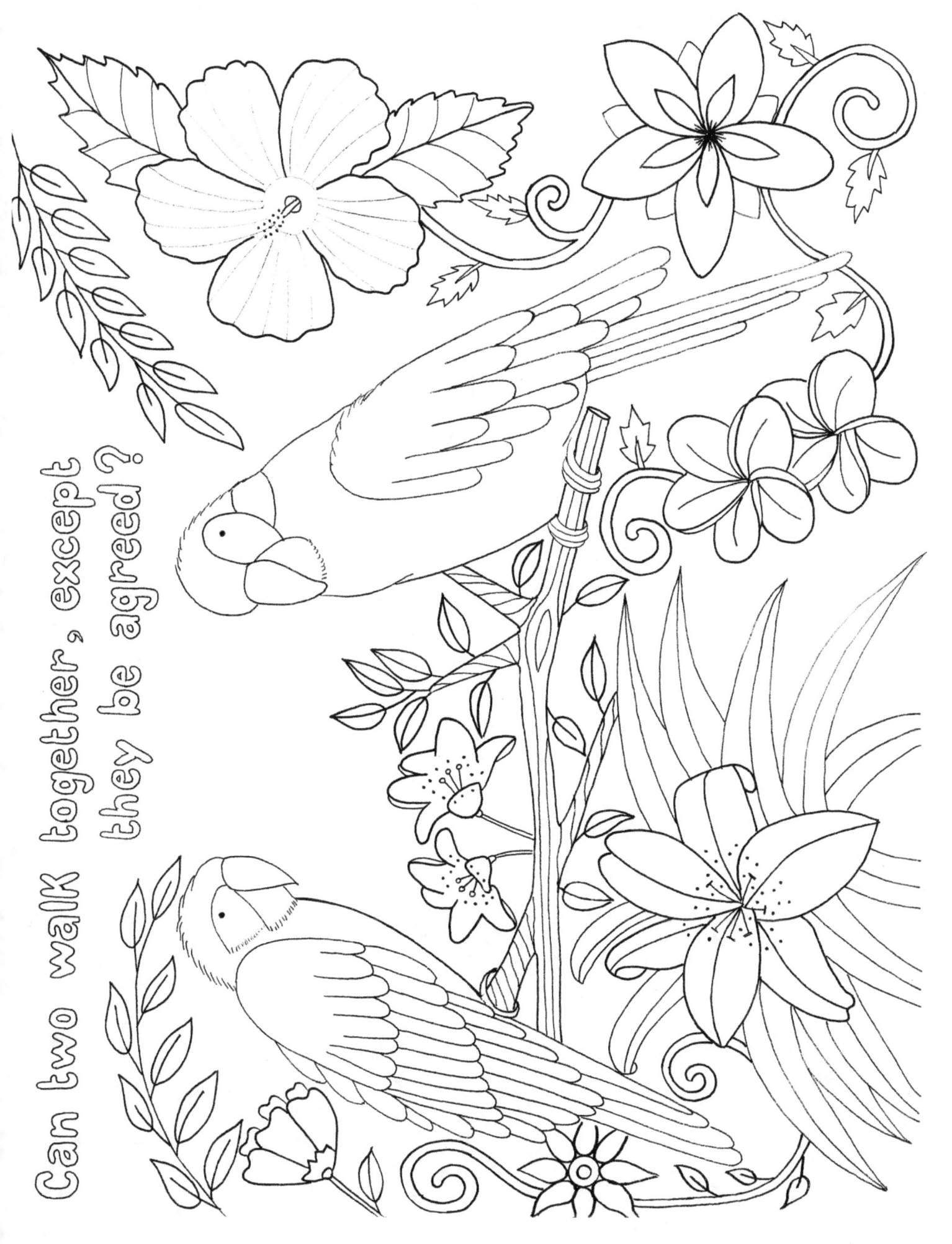

Can two walk together, except they be agreed?

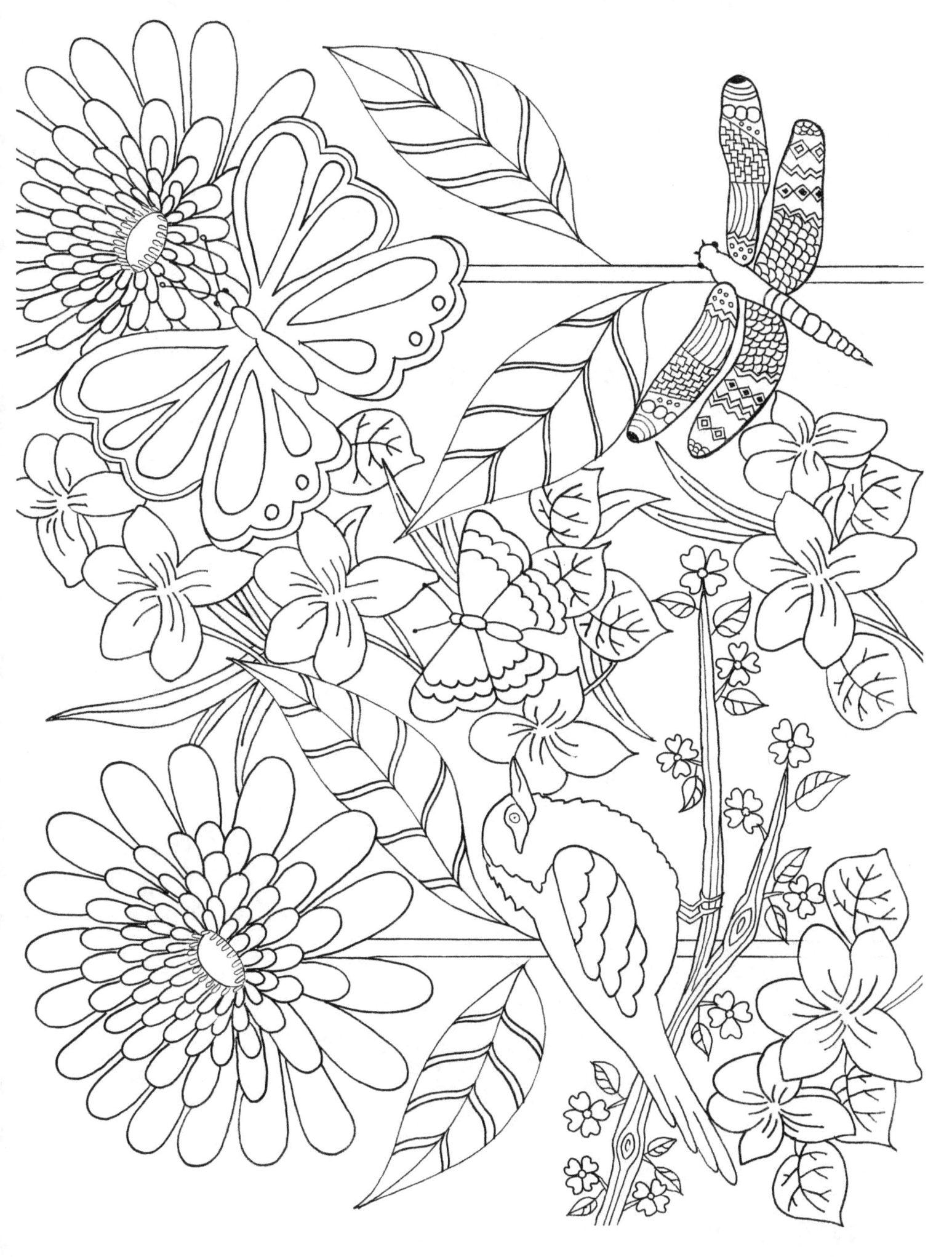

www.ingramcontent.com/pod-product-compliance
Lightning Source LLC
Chambersburg PA
CBHW081120180526
45170CB00008B/2943